Praise for THE *Revolutio*

For far too long, we've heard the "future of
to radically change. In *The Revolution of Work*, ... why work
is ripe for a revolution and what you can do to propel your
organization into the future. As a fellow HR executive, I believe
everyone in HR has something to learn from Anessa's experiences
and work she has done in our industry. If you're ready to be
challenged and take a hard look at your organization and your own
actions, this is the book for you. Anessa's honesty and directness is
downright refreshing and deeply needed. It's time to make real change
at work and build better workplaces for the future—workplaces that
demand inclusion for all.

Hebba Youssef
Chief People Officer,
Founder and Creator of *I Hate It Here* Newsletter

Anessa Fike's *The Revolution of Work: Fuck the Patriarchy and the
Workplace It Built* is not just a critique but a professional and personal
perspective on the systems that fail the non-majority. Fike's bold,
brilliant, and badass approach, infused with her authentic voice that
doesn't shy away from a curse word or two or three, speaks directly
to the reader. It's a conversation and a call to action. A push to use
our voices, power, and privilege to challenge the status quo and strive
for a more equitable workplace in a way that only Anessa can do. If
you are looking for a view of the current workplace from a truth-
teller's perspective, you don't want to pass this up. If you aren't
looking for that type of read, this book was actually written for you.
Read it anyway.

Rocki Howard
Founder and Chief Diversiologist,
Diversiology.io

This book explores what many of us are thinking but are too afraid to talk about. And they are conversations that need to be had. I love the diversity of topics, insights, and practical takeaways that you can apply or think about in your day-to-day life. It's raw and honest and gets straight to the point. It reminds us that in order to reach a work utopia, we need to get comfortable being uncomfortable. We need more truth tellers like Anessa—that's the only way a revolution of work will be successful. It's time to shake things up, and I can't think of a better book to shift the narrative about where we are today and where we need to get to. This is a must read!

Alex Seiler
Chief People Officer and Start-Up Advisor

"When I ask my son, who is a part of Generation Alpha, what a boss or a CEO looks like, he tells me, 'You, Mama. You're a boss.'" Anessa Fike's *The Revolution of Work: Fuck the Patriarchy and the Workplace It Built* reads like a chat over drinks with your friend—one who happens to be Anessa. She fearlessly dishes out critiques and liberally drops expletives because sometimes you have to say what you have to say. The book reads as if she's casually sharing experiences involving oppressive workplace norms, their impact, and why they've been tolerated for far too long. Brace yourself for an unfiltered, candid dialogue as she pushes for a workplace revolution that's long overdue. In this read, she is the Boss.

Torin Ellis
Principal, Diversity Strategist, and Culture Creator,
The Torin Ellis Brand, torinellis.com

In *The Revolution of Work*, Anessa Fike fearlessly navigates the intricate landscape of workplace dynamics, drawing on her authentic experiences to shed light on the urgent need for transformation. As a fellow author, HR executive, and friend, I find her assertive yet conversational tone relatable and refreshing. Anessa's disruptive approach to dismantling patriarchal norms challenges our thinking and sparks essential conversations about reshaping work environments. Her manifesto is a call to arms and an invitation to embark on a collective journey toward more equitable and humane workplaces. It's a testament to her passion, authenticity, and commitment to fostering positive change in the professional realm.

Jessica D. Winder,
Chief People Officer
and author of *The Hidden Gem Within*

The "future of work" was yesterday, and it failed employees and workplace cultures alike. It's now time for a Revolution of Work that pushes us to upend everything we think we know about workplaces and business. Many of the processes People professionals follow haven't been intentionally updated in decades! This book shatters those outdated practices and pushes leaders and Talent professionals to really see the inequities they've helped create. But more importantly, it urges them to revolutionize and intentionally build all those systems anew. Adding this book to your best practices toolkit will help you push past performative and harmful People and business practices and build more thoughtful and equitable workplaces. Whether you are a People professional, a manager, an executive, or an individual contributor, this book will help you see how the patriarchy and its many inequitable systems, processes, and policies affect everything we know, think, and do about work…and once you see it, you simply can't go back.

Daniela (Dani) Herrera,
Talent and DEI Consultant,
deibydani.com

The very phrase "future of work" conjures up academics and Wall Street pundits jousting with charts and data focused on macro trends into the next decade. It's a term that suggests something too big to be seen or too ephemeral to be felt by people who are doing the actual working. That's why this book is revelatory. It isn't some set of big ideas designed to be a future cover story on Fast Company. It is the future of work as seen by people making that future happen. It is a hands-dirty, frontlines POV of all the ways you'll find work to be broken, and a personal challenge for you (yes, you) to make it better. This is a worthwhile read for leaders, HR professionals, managers, and anyone who cares about how we spend so much of our waking lives.

James Ellis,
Chief Brander, Employer Brand Labs,
employerbrandlabs.com

When I first read Anessa Fike's *The Revolution of Work: Fuck the Patriarchy and the Workplace It Built*, I felt like I was talking to a friend at work who was hell-bent on really changing what everyone keeps talking about—the future of work. Many people talk about the future, but few are ready to share how to change it so that we are all able to have an equitable and fair experience in the workplace. It takes a true leader to be able to highlight why we need a revolution at work, and Anessa is the perfect human being to speak truth in her power-smart, thoughtful, keenly observant, and generous way with a force of commitment to justice under her cape. Anessa's book and work is about getting shit done so we can all thrive.

T. Tara Turk,
Writer, DEI and Talent Executive,
Founder of Equity Activations, equityactivations.com

THE *Revolution* OF WORK

FUCK

THE *Patriarchy* AND THE WORKPLACE IT BUILT

ANESSA FIKE

Editors: Laurie Knight and Erin Tackitt
Cover Design by: Kristina Edstrom

An Imprint for GracePoint Publishing (www.GracePointPublishing.com)

GracePoint Matrix, LLC
624 S. Cascade Ave, Suite 201
Colorado Springs, CO 80903
www.GracePointMatrix.com
Email: Admin@GracePointMatrix.com
SAN # 991-6032

A Library of Congress Control Number has been requested and is pending.

ISBN: (Paperback) 978-1-961347-54-0
eISBN: 978-1-961347-55-7

Books may be purchased for educational, business, or sales promotional use.
For bulk order requests and price schedule contact:
Orders@GracePointPublishing.com

Dedication

To all of those in the world, trying every day to make a difference and an impact for the greater good, including but not limited to the following people who I want to thank for existing: to my wonderful husband, who is an active ally, my best friend, and my support system through every step of life; to my son, who is one of the kindest, most inclusive, brilliant, and most artistic souls on our planet; to my parents who always told me that I could be anything that I wanted to be and to never ever let myself think I couldn't do what a man could do, only better; to my fierce and bold friends—you know who you are—that are both inside and outside of the HR and People space; and lastly, to every People, Talent, and Culture person out there working to try to make work less damn horrible.

Table of Contents

Introduction

Work is broken. It is so broken that in Gallup's State of the Global Workplace: 2023 Report, we learned that only 23 percent of the world's employees were engaged in 2022.[1]

When you talk to as many people about work every day as I do, across organizations, levels, regions, industries, and countries, you start to see trends. You see people hating Monday morning and letting that despair and sorrow creep into Sunday. You hear of debilitating stress on the minds and stress living in the bodies of many, an increase in mental health issues that companies don't give employees the time and grace to sort out, and a massive amount of frustration.

And this isn't even just frustration seen from the employee side. Employers should be heavily worried, too, since the Gallup report also stated that employees who are not engaged or who are actively *disengaged* cost the world $8.8 trillion in lost productivity in 2022 (equal to 9 percent of the global gross domestic product).

So, why do we think work is working?

I want this book to spur a movement. I want this book to allow you to push past the veils to see what is really happening, why it is happening, and why it is so detrimental to people. And I want you to join us in doing something about it. With just one person, change can be hard and difficult, but with hundreds of thousands, even millions of people all pushing a movement forward, well, just imagine what we can shift for the way our children and our children's children can work.

And by the way, this book will not be like every other human resources, culture, or business book you've read. In fact, it may seem like you're talking to a confidant, a friend, or someone you trust to see you, and all in a very conversational tone because I'm nothing if not authentic wherever I am in this world: on stages, chatting with friends,

---

[1] https://www.gallup.com/workplace/349484/state-of-the-global-workplace.aspx

Anessa Fike

working with my teams, mentoring others, or talking with family. I want, from deep within my bones, to change the way we work. I also have a real problem with authority and how things "have always been done" because I think mechanisms of the patriarchy and an imbalance of power dynamics hinder the way we all work. So this book will seem disruptive in its structure. That's on purpose. Huge props to my amazing publishers at GracePoint Publishing and for the Women Empower X Imprint for allowing me the latitude to try something outside of the way "things are normally done" in the world of traditional book publishing.

The concept of the future of work has been rooted in reiterating existing processes and only tweaking items that have, at their core, been in place for decades if not more. My concept, The Revolution of Work, is about doing more and actually creating lasting change so that the workplace reflects everyone's wishes and well-being. The future of work is still deeply set in the patriarchy. The Revolution of Work is about tearing down current workplace processes, starting again from scratch, and implementing equitable solutions to build on.

Chapter 1

WHY NOW?

Before I decided that I wanted to write a book about work, I had always wanted to write. Even as I was thinking about what to major in during my pre-college and even my college years, I often wondered what my *job*, what my *work life*, would look like.

I pictured myself working at some fashion magazine, haute couture preferred, every day waltzing into a beautiful glass skyscraper, looking perfectly polished, wearing designer shoes, an expensive purse on my arm, and sitting down at my desk to write a blurb about upcoming trends. My fellow millennials know what I'm talking about: *The Devil Wears Prada* was a definite staple in the movies of our youth.

Yet, I had no idea then how much that storyline and the aspects of the characters would come into my life.

Let me take you back, where my *professional* life began…

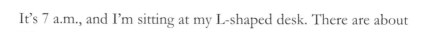

It's 7 a.m., and I'm sitting at my L-shaped desk. There are about fifteen other people sitting at their desks around me.

My computer, quite honestly the same model used in my middle school computer class, sits on my desk, complete with a keyboard in front of me that no one would even consider calling off-white since it's been used and dirtied over the years. I hear fingers flying across the keyboards around me, and the noise is multiplied by the number of people.

Murmurs of voices also circle my ears as people have multiple conversations in different areas of the office, loud enough to hear but quiet enough to miss distinguishable words. Camera flashes and clicks from the photo department nestle in the background.

The office is an open environment, which works well when we yell across desks and run back and forth when we need to, and that happens often. The lighting is the same yellow-and-orange-tinged glow that was used in the 1970s, and it's likely that it hasn't been changed since. The desks are made of cheap, wood-esque surfaced particle board, the likes of which tell you it was made to look like real wood grain but not actually resemble wood in any other way. The carpet is honestly less memorable, probably some sort of gray or brown that was cheap when they installed it.

Cigarette smoke wafts through the room, which says the publisher is in the building and has been for about as long as it has taken the smoke to move from his office back down the hallway and up to my desk area. Mixed with the stuffiness of the old heating system that dried out my skin in the winter, and the barely-there air-conditioning that cranked out as much as it could in the summer, the smoke and the never-quite-correct temperature made for interesting bedfellows.

In the little office behind me and to the right, our editor is screaming the name of one of our reporters in a tone that seems like he is in trouble. The back-and-forth between this particular reporter and our editor goes on for about forty-five minutes on and off over the duration of most mornings. More frequently than not, doors slam and the tension-filled voices of the two rise above the level of acceptable office volume. Sometimes, the assistant editor jumps into the mix. And undoubtedly there are a few colorful words like *fuck* and *son of a bitch* thrown around.

This was the setting of my first professional job out of college. I was a newspaper reporter for a then-family-owned newspaper in North Carolina. The editor was the first woman the newspaper had ever had in that position, and I can visualize her red, flushed face like it was yesterday. I can also hear her voice in my ear, a voice that was like nails on a chalkboard. She was my own louder, less chic version of Meryl Streep in *The Devil Wears Prada*.

What you may not see in my description above are the eggshells we all had to figuratively walk on when we entered the building every day. Or the stress of trying to be creative daily on deadline so that the paper could get out of our hands in the newsroom by

8:30 a.m. on the dot to go to the printers in the back. Or the desk setup where the assistant editors were staring at all of our reporter screens, nearly breathing over our shoulders as we typed that day's news. Or the tears streaming down our faces as we hovered in the pastel-tiled bathrooms after the stripping of dignity and outright verbal takedowns the editor doled out in team meetings.

This was my workplace, one so rooted in old-school patriarchy that I smelled it wafting up the hallways in the smoke from the cigarettes of its prodigal son.

I was paid $24,000 a year to work five days a week for fourteen to sixteen hours a day plus one Saturday a month for six to eight hours. Boil that down and it's about $6/hour, all requiring a four-year college degree of course.

My desk wasn't aesthetically pleasing, and neither was the office. The work hours ran afoul of my own natural circadian rhythm, and the mentorship and camaraderie came from other reporters in the trenches with me because it wasn't at all coming from the newsroom leadership.

But day after day, for nearly two years, my brain was expected to be in tip-top creative shape to consistently churn out copy, all for the betterment of the newspaper owners' pockets. And we were all expected to dress like we were entering a courtroom at any time, which is to say, dresses or suits for women, with closed toe, heeled shoes and pantyhose, of course. Never mind times like when I had to trudge through a wheat field as I was interviewing the local hog farmer for a story; the pantyhose and heels were still a requirement.

I didn't realize it then, but looking back now, I was great at my job despite the professional handcuffs and deep-rooted patriarchal grasp. Heck, I even won a press award during my time there.

If I had thought about it more then—and to be fair, I didn't have much brain space to do anything else back then, given the hours and exhaustion—I'd have realized it was a toxic work environment.

I just knew I had to get out of there, or I'd lose myself.

This was my workplace, one so rooted in old-school patriarchy that I smelled it wafting up the hallways in the smoke from the cigarettes of its prodigal son.

That was more than fifteen years ago. When I think about that time in my life and how I fell into human resources (HR) after that, I wonder if my horrible experience didn't push me in the direction of trying to make workplaces better so no one had to experience such a workplace again.

Today, it's a chilly, rainy day in mid-November as I sit in my home by the gas fireplace, an oat milk latte in my favorite mug in hand, ready to embark on this journey of writing a book. There is a TV show playing. Creativity and productivity, for me, stem from familiar places, and while sitting in front of a TV with a laptop may not be the ideal workplace for some people to bear productive thoughts, it is for me. My hair is a mess (I didn't brush it today, shocker!), my attire is a classic sweatshirt and sweatpants set, and my shoes of choice are Minnetonka slippers. My contacts aren't in my eyes, and I have no makeup on. Instead, I am wearing eyeglasses that slip off if I tilt my head too far down too quickly. The kitchen is close by with snacks, and one of my prized possessions and COVID-pandemic purchases—an espresso machine—sits close enough that I'm sure I have way more caffeine in the mornings than one person should.

This is my ideal working environment.

I go outside for walks when it's nice out, but I don't have to get in my car and drive anywhere. I don't have to jump on the train barreling toward my stop by an office.

Quite frankly, I don't even have to wear a bra if I don't want to.

My wants and needs for what work and work environment look like have changed over the years for a few reasons: different stages of life, health reasons, and the shift from life engulfed by work to life that includes it. And I keep refining, preparing to shift into another stage when needed.

I'm a "knowledge worker," which means that my work comes from previous experience and expertise, and I strategically lead organizations on the People side of their businesses. Therefore, my job doesn't force me to be at a specific or particular location to do that. Whether I have gray hair, purple hair, platinum hair, or all of the above, my work doesn't hinge on what I look like, but instead is based on what is in my brain. I am privileged in that; the whiteness of my skin has allowed me to pick and choose more opportunities coming my way, opportunities I'm fully aware most people do not get. But I want to continue to do my part to change that.

This book is about how work dominates aspects of human lives, even more than we can fathom. It's about how the dynamics of power and patriarchy filter through the many interactions and instances that happen to people in the span of a workday, and how those elements compound over time to make work more of a hindrance than a benefit.

I mean, you never hear people say, "Damn, the weekend is coming? Really? Already?" There's a reason for that.

It's about showcasing the elements that just don't work for people today so we can name them and dismantle them to create healthy and happy workplaces where all humans can thrive. It's a mission so near and dear to my heart that I made it the mission of my company, Fike + Co, a decade ago. And we've helped more than one-hundred organizations on that path in those ten years since.

But this book isn't going to be like any other book you have read in the HR or business space. You won't see an aggregate of other people's stories thrown in here with only minimal words from me; in fact, you'll hear some of my own stories along the way— times when I had to look across at my trusted colleagues, friends, and leaders and say, "Am I the only one seeing this?" You won't read tons and tons of data and statistics from study upon study that I have done; I am not a research scientist or a social psychologist, and it's best I leave those items for them.

But what you will read in this book are elements that I have found are tied to how and why the patriarchy set up work to work for them and to maintain power and wealth, and very little of that has changed in today's work structure. You will also find that I will push the thinking of those who have been so rigidly stuck in what "work" looks like that they haven't taken the time to think outside of that box to the *what ifs*, and you will read trends that I have seen have really horrible impacts on many organizations.

And I hope that what you read makes you shake your head and say, "Yep, I've seen that, too" or "Wow, I feel seen."

I do want to make sure that I also point out that this is not a solutions book. I don't have all of the answers, but I do know what isn't working. I also think that the way each company's culture is set up is so dependent on so many pieces, that making blanket statements about how to set a great culture in place with step-by-step guides wouldn't actually be beneficial. This endeavor to change the way we all work and to set up companies that actually support, develop, value, and enliven people is hard and will take time. But we must decide to

> I mean, you never hear people say, "Damn, the weekend is coming? Really? Already?" There's a reason for that.

do it, and we must decide to start down that path sooner rather than later. And by *we*, I mean you, me, and everyone who truly wants to see a different way of working than what we have today.

As I mentioned, I will push you to expand the horizon of what you know about work (or what you *think* you know). I will push you to tear down the parameters set by some old white guys hundreds of years ago and think instead about how we set up a workplace to *benefit* humans instead of stripping workplaces dry of any humanity. I will push you to be more creative, to think through how we might accomplish something different, instead of just saying that "it can't be done" or that "it's hard." I'll also give you a few ideas of places to start from with tiny seeds of thought to spur other ideas that may embrace all lived experiences.

And as we dive in, I will show you first just how truly messed up workplaces are. Sometimes in telling the tales about my frustration of work, workplaces, and leaders that do not get it, I've used expletives. These cuss words are part of how I speak in everyday life, and as I mentioned earlier, I'm the same person at home as I am out with friends or speaking at a conference in front of strangers. This book is not ghostwritten. Every word in this book is mine and mine alone. But I use real words that mean to drive change. And sometimes to drive change, we have to be fucking fed up enough to do something.

There will be many people who say that being nice and kind will change more minds. I've heard it time and time again in my career. "Don't you know that you'll attract more flies with honey?"

Well, when the flies start carrying big bags of cash around, telling other flies how to work, and all along stacking the deck to only benefit themselves, I'd like to honestly squash those flies. The time for honey is gone. Hand me the vinegar. In fact, hand me the gasoline. And if you throw in a lighter, I might take that, too.

Now is the time to be real and to absolutely throw out the status quo. It's been around and alive for far too long, and it's served far too little of humanity. The status quo must go.

Work is a problem for many. Large corporations exist that are too huge to completely change overnight, but change is possible. And it may take years to pivot to that, but the idea is to start trying now.

Service and on-site-based industries like healthcare, hospitality, manufacturing, and education are all harder to change because of the work they do, who they serve, and what shift and coverage dynamics are at play; yet, I think that even there, we can make changes and tweaks to allow humans to be more engaged and more fulfilled in their work. We just have to stop putting thoughts into a structure that exists now, tear that down, and get creative enough to pilot something new.

In this book, however, I'm going to focus mostly on knowledge-based work and those environments because those industries have the ability to change at a much faster pace than others. When I say *knowledge-based work*, I'm referring to work that can be done mostly through emails, calls, and meetings, and is based on the employee pulling expertise and cognitive thinking ability from their brain to do their job.

This book is also not a book on inclusion, disability, equity, diversity, justice, or accessibility as there are amazing books by other authors that are centered in this work. There are places in this book where I will mention my own white privilege and the privilege of others because those are important factors in moving through what's wrong with our working world today and how we can make it better for all humans—not just those who look like me. There are some inter-

> The time for honey is gone. Hand me the vinegar. In fact, hand me the gasoline. And if you throw in a lighter, I might take that, too.

woven ties, causes, and effects in all work—and some of us have more influence to change those things in our current society than others and shouldn't take that lightly. Diversity, equity, inclusivity, justice, accessibility, and belonging should be in every piece and all roles of an organization, not just centered on a few people in one department; and those elements should be thought about with each business decision a leader makes.

When we look at the ways in which work isn't working for everyone today, we have to make note of the patriarchy's part in it. Our entire country—the United States of America—was created for the benefit of one demographic in particular, and the rules, regulations, and ways of business have had to shift only slightly over the years for that same demographic to keep the power and wealth. But it's not pie, and allowing others who aren't white men to work in an environment that treats them well and leaves them fulfilled shouldn't be as hard as it is today. We can all succeed. Although we have worked with companies that have offices all around the world, I'll be focusing on the United States because we have a lot of work to do in our country in lots of areas, including how to dismantle the malicious white supremacy and patriarchy that exists as the default in the everyday life of American citizens.

This book is meant to spark a revolution. My hope is that this book becomes a touchstone on your bookshelf, and you use it as a guide throughout your career to come back to often, whether to feel less isolated, or to feel seen or heard, or even to share and drive conversation. With that, as years go on and we continue to learn more about various People topics, the language in this book may become outdated. That's okay. We should want to continue to learn. Please give this book the same grace we give ourselves when we are trying to learn new and better ways to use language and talk about all things that revolve around people in our society.

And if you are a white person reading this book and find parts that make you uncomfortable, please take a moment, look over your own actions and biases, and then I'll humbly ask you to consider what makes you mad or defensive about it before moving to the next section. The way we work today was set up to work for white men specifically. It was set up in a time when white men (*only* white men) held power and wealth, and the way we now work hasn't changed much in all of those years.

I truly believe that we, as humans, can do better, especially at something we spend about a third of our lives doing.

The human brain really wants us to put things into nice, neat little boxes—it's our way of rationalizing the outside world. And it's tough to shake ourselves out of the world we know, even if it isn't working for us. We try to fit everything into a box that has already been created and labeled. We try to make sense of the things that seem complicated by putting them close to or in with that which looks or sounds or seems similar.

These are all natural ways the human brain functions. But, sometimes, we need to completely smash the boxes that were put in place and start again.

And that's exactly what needs to happen with work—especially in America where our corporate culture is such that we strive to hustle and grind, even when it is killing us. Americans want to be the best at everything, but to our own detriment. We need to really look around at ourselves and at the rest of the world and say, "work isn't working anymore."

Big things take time, and they take intentionality. We will not change work if we are all fine with it not working. We must decide to change it.

Work has been broken for far too long. It is time for the Revolution of Work. The ill-fitting system that has only consistently benefited a few demographic subsets must change.

The time for that change is now.

Chapter 2

THE REVOLUTION OF WORK
VERSUS
THE FUTURE OF WORK

I was so excited.

I'd finally gotten up the nerve to ask my boss for professional development money because I wanted to attend my first HR conference.

I'd just started in the HR field, and I wanted to go learn, to open my mind for what could be, what we could do as HR professionals, and how we (I!) could change people's lives at work.

So the morning of the first day of the session, I woke up early, I dressed in my best work attire, complete with new flat shoes that were on trend for the season (you can never really take the fashion girlie out of the woman), and I felt hopeful and confident as I stepped out the door.

The conference was local, and it was put on by one of the top certifying organizations of the industry. For anyone in the HR industry, you have likely heard or will hear that many seasoned HR professionals say that this organization is made up of dinosaurs. You may have even heard or will hear people call them greedy and out of touch. I tend to agree, now.

But at the time, I had no idea. I wanted to research the top organization doing what seemed like the most *professional* work in the space, and they were touted as *it!*

Early to rise, I set myself up for success! I was excited to elevate my knowledge about our industry space and excited to meet others who shared my passion for it. I drove over to the conference center, mentally checking off internal goals for the day, then I parked, grabbed my coffee, and headed inside.

Being new to the industry, I didn't know anyone. Searching the throngs of people, I observed others as I walked to the registration table to pick up my badge. That day, I'd be an observer more than anything. Deciding which room and which talk interested me most, I continued in and took a seat at the back of the first session I chose.

I was in my early career, in my early twenties, and I had so many ideas bouncing in my head for what I might hear that day from professionals, industry leaders, and people who, to me, knew a *helluva* lot more about HR than I did.

When the first session's speaker stood up, people applauded. I had my notebook out, ready to take down notes fastidiously. My mind was a sponge waiting to soak it all up.

But then the speaker opened their mouth. And what came out was a straight condemnation and vilification of the millennial generation; the one I am a part of, by the way.

She said that millennials didn't know how to work, that we didn't understand the value of a dollar, that we wanted to be babied, that we were born with silver spoons in our mouths, that we were the participation trophy generation, that we didn't know how to figure anything out and probably weren't smart enough to anyway, and on and on.

I looked around. No one had stunned looks on their faces like I did. No one else's jaw was on the floor like mine. I then noticed that every other person in the room was at least a good decade older than me and nodding their heads in agreement.

I felt my face flush, and the rage inside of me burned. That speaker didn't know me. She didn't know my ambition, my work ethic, what I had accomplished, or really anything about any millennial it seemed. At least not the ones I know.

But there she was, an *expert* or a *thought leader*, and she was spewing hatred about an *entire* generation at hundreds of agreeing people in an industry meant to *help* humans in the workplace.

WHAT?!

I didn't sit through the rest of the conference. In fact, I stood right up, did not try to be quiet as I left, and slammed the door as I walked right to the conference organizers to tell them how disappointing it was to be a part of such a bitter and dismissive organization that made me pay to be at a conference where I was belittled. One of the ladies looked me right in the eyes after I told them how I felt, and told them that they shouldn't be having so-called experts like this, and she said, "Well, that's been my experience so far with millennials, too, so maybe she has a point?"

I then asked her how many millennials she worked with.

She said, "Four."

And I said, "Well, then maybe you should look past your prejudices, stop discriminating against a younger generation that you should be mentoring, developing, and even learning new technologies from, and seek out to work with more than four before you denounce an entire new group of working people."

She stared at me, mouth wide open, blankly, with nothing more to say, so I walked away.

I haven't gone to another one of that organization's conferences since.

But this is how our workplace has gotten so fucked up. People like that perpetuate lies which people presume are based on some sort of research but aren't.

We work with one or two people, think we know everything there is to know about them, put them in boxes, and forget how to be humans. Do we really want to be a part of this? Do we really want to perpetuate such blatant untruths?

Oh, and by the way, the horrible speaker? She was talking about the future of work.

Yes, I know.

It isn't quite the *future of work* if you don't have anyone to work in the next ten years and you denounce those who will be the bulk of the workforce by then.

People across business love to call innovation in the HR, Culture, and People space the future of work, almost as if they each get dibs on a brand-new self-driving flying car every time they use the phrase.

That phrase? We've been using it for a decade. When you look back and really think about it—has work gotten better in that time?

No! It's gotten worse!

Employee reports of work stress were at an all-time high[2] in the most recent decades, according to Gallup's 2022[3] and 2023 State of the Global Workplace Reports.[4] And we don't even have the full report about how people thought about the whole of 2023 yet.

The *future of work* is old, it's passed, and it is so tired a phrase that it doesn't even really have any meaning left anymore. Truly. Anytime I see someone use this term, I know three things: 1) that person actually has no idea about how to push the People and HR industries forward; 2) the person is out of touch with the day-to-day employee experiences of people; and 3) the person is trying too hard and not succeeding in being innovative and relevant.

Even this definition by McKinsey leaves nearly everything to the imagination because this is, to me, full of a bunch of words and not much substance: "The future of work refers to an informed perspective on what businesses and other organizations need to know about how work could shift (given digitization and other

---

[2] https://www.cnbc.com/2022/08/12/job-unhappiness-is-at-a-staggering-all-time-high-according-to-gallup.html

[3] https://www.cca-global.com/content/latest/article/2023/05/state-of-the-global-workplace-2022-report-346/

[4] https://www.gallup.com/workplace/349484/state-of-the-global-work place.aspx

trends), plus how workforces and workplaces can prepare for those changes, big and small."[5]

Basically, it says the future of the work is the future. Well, duh. Thanks for that amazingly helpful and super articulate description, McKinsey! (Note the sarcasm.)

For me, those who tout *future of work* are those who are clawing so heavily for their own relevance, almost trying to repurpose things that they have used in the past and trying to make them fit again in the future—like bringing '90s fashion back. Some of it may work, sure, but let's be fair, no one wants the equivalent of low-rise jeans with whale tails again. It was bad even the first time around, and I feel the same about a lot of the programs, trends, and ideas that come out of the future-of-work discussions.

And to be fair, the bulk of what is said on the HR stages about the future of work is better left unsaid because it bores to sleep those of us who are actually doing progressive shit in these HR streets.

We have been doing knowledge work the same since the 1950s. The nine-to-five was used then to help farmers align work with the sunshine, and then when the Industrial Revolution came along, corporate America as we know it started and followed suit. If you think about it, even our school systems, daycares, and most businesses operate very closely to that nine-to-five structure. But why?

For the first time in history, we have five generations in the workforce, from the traditionalists (born 1925 to 1945) to baby boomers (born 1946 to 1964), to Generation X (born 1965 to 1980), then millennials (born 1981 to 2000), and finally Generation Z (born beginning in 2001).[6] In the next few years, we could

---

[5] https://www.mckinsey.com/featured-insights/mckinsey-explainers/what-is-the-future-of-work

[6] https://www.purdueglobal.edu/education-partnerships/generational-workforce-differences-infographic/

even see a sixth generation entering the workforce, even just in family businesses or as interns or apprentices, as early Generation Alpha (born 2010 to 2024) members start to enter their teen years.[7]

The youngest generations are fighting the way things have always been done, as they should. Generation Z is demanding more humanity, growth, pay, and freedom *from* work while taking less crap; again, as they should.

If work takes up 2,000 hours or more of our time every year (which for full-time workers is about 23 percent of our lives just with a forty-hour workweek), then we should be able to adjust and adapt it like we do other aspects of our lives, like our health and wellness. Work should be a lot closer to a lifestyle choice since it takes up a third of life, and it will need to continue to be a choice as we venture into the next ten to twenty years and beyond.

Generation Z and the generations to follow aren't going to fit into the box that was constructed long before them—the box that was then patched up and reinforced despite the wear and tear and held up with duct tape ever since. They want to break out of the box. Hell, there doesn't even need to be a semblance or a thought of a box around them at all. And they'd actually much prefer it that way. Like generations before them, they want to make a name for themselves in ways that are unique to their world views and their myriad of lived experiences.

And by the way, Generation Z is the most racially and ethnically diverse generation to ever enter the workforce in the US, with 48 percent of the generation coming from communities of color, according to NPR.[8] And experts believe Generation Alpha de-

---

[7] https://en.wikipedia.org/wiki/Generation_Alpha

[8] https://www.npr.org/2018/11/15/668106376/generation-z-is-the-most-racially-and-ethnically-diverse-yet

---

Anessa Fike

mographics will be even more diverse than their Generation Z predecessors.

So, this circus we call "work" right now has to change dramatically if organizations actually want to have employees from the Generation Z and Generation Alpha cohorts, and frankly, if they want to continue to have employees from the millennial generation.

Because as a millennial, I can tell you one thing: I'm fucking tired, and I know I'm not the only one.

I'm tired of the patriarchy continuing to tell me and everyone who isn't a white heterosexual cisgender man to work in a certain way and by specific guidelines to the benefit of them but to our detriment. In addition, I'm tired of playing by these outdated rules while being unfairly compensated in comparison to the same white heterosexual cisgender men who made these rules.

I'm tired of the patriarchy setting the rules for a world that doesn't solely look like them and doing it in a country where the majority of the buying power and commercial benefits come from the labor and income of women and non-white people.

I'm tired of the patriarchy and the systems that it put in place being covertly or overtly advantageous for them and their families, and covertly or overtly disadvantageous for those who aren't white men. I'm tired of centering everything around them in order to succeed. I'm tired of the seemingly endless number of white men who fail forward, despite horrible leadership and decision-making. I'm tired of story after story of white men behaving badly and not enough of them being held to any measure of accountability that would actually allow them to learn a lesson or two that they so desperately need to just be decent humans.

I'm tired of those with disabilities, those with neurodivergence, women, nonbinary folx, transgender humans, members of the LGBTQIA+ communities, Black, Brown, Asian, and Indigenous people, and any other historically marginalized or under-represented group (URGs) all having to work harder in varying capacities just to make a fraction of the pay white men make.

I'm tired of intersectionality being society's exception instead of the rule. As humans, we are complex, complicated, and nuanced individuals, and we shouldn't be put in a box. In fact, we shouldn't have to choose one box that feels like it only sort of fits. We should be figuring out how to throw the boxes out completely and looking at the person in front of us, fully and openly. We are all unique human beings, yet society rewards the vanilla, the shirts and ties, and the khaki brigades of the world. (And if you don't think people do this, white men and even white women have seen URGs as monoliths for years, while also saying that they themselves are not monoliths. Hypocrites? You make that call. No, just kidding— they are!)

I'm tired of all of the stories that I and my fellow HR and People colleagues have witnessed, been exposed to, or even fallen victim to that involve leaders in organizations that do despicable and horrible things without any semblance of consequence, and while completely blind to the inappropriateness of it all.

I'm tired of those people (read: white people) who say they "don't see color," are "colorblind," "worked their way to the top," and every other ridiculous excuse that just makes that particular person feel superior in any way they can cling to, without ever having to do any actual work on themselves by looking inward.

I'm tired of people being interrupted in meetings, mostly by those who tend not to have their own original ideas so they steal from others, or being interrupted by those who have had way more privilege than anyone else in the room could even fathom.

I'm tired of society and the working world seeing vulnerability and humanity as weaknesses.

I'm tired of performance reviews that are tied to mechanisms of control (purposefully or not) to hold back and control other demographics.

I'm tired of women and nonbinary folx being told to dull their sparkle while men are told that they are ambitious and have leadership qualities.

I'm tired of women being told that they are too bold or too direct. I'm tired of women being measured during performance reviews on a scale by which history tells us only rewards male-dominated characteristics and leaves female-dominated characteristics out of the conversation completely or graded differently.

I'm tired of society also seeing confidence as fine for men but too boisterous for women.

I'm tired of companies thinking that men make better leaders than women, even though every ounce of data shows the contrary.

I'm tired of investors thinking men make better investments than women, even though, again, every ounce of data shows the contrary.

> I'm tired of women and nonbinary folx being told to dull their sparkle while men are told that they are ambitious and have leadership qualities.

I'm so extremely fucking tired that it irks me to even have to write that companies tout DEIJ (diversity, equity, inclusion, and justice) practices but 99 percent of them just want to *say* they are doing things instead of actually doing the work.

I'm tired of our country defaulting to Christian beliefs. We are a country made up of people from all over the world who have come here to make a home for themselves and their families—and Christianity, while one of the largest religions, isn't the *only* religion. Yet, we center it in the US—so much so that people tell me, "Happy Easter" as I'm writing this chapter, and I'm agnostic. If we truly want to be inclusive and intersectional, we'd center all religions in the US as much as we do Christianity. We should see way more "Eid Mubarak" messages, more "Shana Tova," more "Happy Vesak Day," more "Sending you warm wishes for a joyful Kwanzaa," more "Happy Winter Solstice," and more "May you have a lovely Diwali." And we should also be more inclusive by being open to those who are more spiritual than religious, or those who prefer atheist or agnostic practices.

I'm tired of work centering white-washed holidays like Columbus Day, Thanksgiving Day, and Fourth of July. How many hand turkeys can elementary school kids make before we talk about the actual killings that happened to the Indigenous people over the "happy" Thanksgiving cornucopias? We should see more people prioritize Juneteenth over July 4th because that is the day that all Americans were freed by government decree, though some enslaved Black Americans were still not free by that day. Celebrating Fourth of July may signify to your Black employees and colleagues that you care less about them than you do their white counterparts, which is the same thing that celebrating Thanksgiving may show your Indigenous friends.

And if you're tired of these things, too, and other ridiculous practices, comments, behaviors, and power dynamics that the patriarchy wants us to believe are just the way it is, then this Revolution of Work movement is for you.

If you've ever felt like work wasn't working for you, this book is for you.

If you've ever felt like your voice didn't matter as much as others in your work environment, if you've ever looked around and realized there weren't any or as many people who *looked* like you in your workplace, and if you've ever had to "code switch" where you put on a mask for work because it is safer or easier than showing your authentic self or true cultural background, then this book is for you.

If you've ever been ousted by a company simply for using your voice and standing proud for who you are, and if you've ever nearly lost yourself because of your work or because of your work environment, and if you've ever been *so* fucking tired and so fucking frustrated about work in today's society, then this book is definitely for you.

If you've ever looked around and thought to yourself, *Work is rigged for white people to succeed*, this book is for you.

If you identify as a white man (and by the way, when I say "white man" or "white men" in this book, I'm referring to white heterosexual cisgender men), then this book is still for you, but only if you are willing to explore your own privilege and your own advantages, while looking at how your interactions may have helped or hurt others by either feeding into patriarchal elements or fighting against them. There is a place for you in the Revolution of Work, but in order to have that place, you need to help work against a system that has actively disadvantaged others, and you must do that through your own actions. We need allies in this space. We need you to poke your head up, look around, and see how the current state of work is very much *not* working for others. And we need *you* to help us change it.

And by the way, before you start to come for me, I don't hate all white men. I'm married to one. I just hate those who continue to hold up the patriarchy, whether they know it or not. (And a good way to know if you are holding up the patriarchy is to ask yourself if you've been an active ally to those who don't look like you in the last week, last month, last year, etc. If the answer is no, or you can't come up with something, then please, start now. Start today. Go educate yourself. And continue reading because there is more on this later.)

Here's the thing: like it or not, in the US, we live in a patriarchal society.

It's been that way since the time of the Founding Fathers—I mean, they were the original white bros and they came over to a country that wasn't theirs to take; they colonized it, and then they said, "Oh, we have what it takes to build a whole nation here."

White guy confidence and all. (Remember, they tend to fail forward in our society the most.)

Now, am I glad that I'm in the US? Yes, I am. Do I wish our history would have gone down differently? Yes, I do. But both things can be true.

James Baldwin said it well: "I love America more than any other country in the world and, exactly for this reason, I insist on the right to criticize her perpetually."

I want us to be so much more, and it's because I care about our country that I want us to be better.

Our society has expressly prohibited anyone that wasn't white or wasn't a hetero cis man from doing pretty much anything except for breathing for the better part of our history (and even allowing breathing can be debated). Honestly, even breathing and existing is hard for some even today, and it's a daily fight against society.

The way we work in the US was set up that way so that American white men could set restrictions in place that helped them succeed and kept others down. They were like, "New nation, who dis?!" And they wanted to showcase what they could do.

But what they probably didn't realize was that we'd be working in pretty much the same way with the same rigid structures nearly 250 years later.

The Industrial Revolution didn't help things—it drove the human element out of business and tried its best to make people work like machines. More profitability. More production. More efficiency. These were the initial driving forces in US business, and it remains so, even today.

> White guy confidence and all. (Remember, they tend to fail forward in our society the most.)

Some of these tenets though are counterintuitive. More profitability in the long term works when you have a stable company that is built on a solid foundation and continues to grow steadily, meaning that for the most part, your people like working with you and they stay. More production in the long term leads to more profitability but there is a tipping point where too much production leads to costly mistakes, some that would likely negate any positive impact you had in the first place. And more efficiency is key until efficiency is the only thing you focus on; efficiency for efficiency's sake doesn't really get anyone anywhere. There needs to also be a strategic plan in place.

So all of these areas that are engrained in our minds of what makes businesses *great*, what makes business leaders *smart*, and what makes people *successful* all stem from a system built by and for white men for other white men, a.k.a. the patriarchy.

In fact, many of us realized that work wasn't working when the COVID-19 pandemic came upon us. We physically and mentally had to shift *how* we worked to remain safe. And there were emotional shifts during that time as well.

Let's think back a moment to the summer of 2019, before we knew that COVID was in our country, and before we knew what it was like in the US to wear masks everywhere we went.

It's a Monday morning, and for most of the continental US, it's probably warm to hot to excruciatingly sizzling in the summer. Most knowledge-worker Americans were slogging their way to the office, many in cities battled throngs of people and traffic to get there on time by 9 a.m. Then, they worked tirelessly at their desks with their laptops or two-screen-setups with several in-person and Zoom meetings sprinkled in, and they packed up their workbag to make the slog home at 5-6 p.m., back through the people and bumper-to-bumper cars.

This way of working—in an office—was "just the way it is," unless you were lucky enough to work for a company that allowed remote working or you worked for yourself.

Then COVID-19 changed the landscape.

The pandemic shifted all of our lives toward a way of being and working that none of us were used to or had ever seen or experienced in our lifetimes. No one ever would have imagined this as part of the future of work. No HR expert at a conference stood up and said that a global pandemic was going to shift how we all worked within a month or two, and for years to come. The future of work, again, was so heavily touted but so brutally off the mark, but we still had to all shift how we were working.

And as knowledge workers, we did work. We didn't stop. We didn't throw up our hands and say, "Well there is no office for me to go to, so I guess I can't do my job."

No, we worked; the way we worked just looked a little different.

There were rumblings at the beginning of COVID about worker productivity, but no one really did much about it because most people thought COVID wouldn't be around long enough to worry about a long-term strategy.

Except some of us *did* think about it.

Those of us in the HR industry who understand human elements foresaw what would happen, and we knew that this pandemic was going to take a while to eradicate, while we unraveled and untangled the mess, on our way back to a "normal" that may be anything but. We told companies to get ready for years, not months, years, that we'd be in the throes of figuring it all out.

Zooms and video calls were the way for many—including back-to-back meetings with little to no downtime in between. And in between those calls were emails and Slack messages, sometimes all three at once.

Oh, and by the way, worker productivity didn't decrease. It actually increased, which quieted some of the naysayers of remote work.

Over the two-plus pandemic years, office working types lived in a sort of limbo with many clinging to the question "When can we get back to the office?" and others realizing that the word *office* is a construct and not necessarily a physical place that was the same for everyone. Employees had created home offices that served them quite well.

Fast-forward to 2023, and we are still having leaders of companies telling people they "have to be in an office."

Seriously? What the actual fuck?! Did they not learn a damn thing during COVID?

Because without an office, they may be asking, *can there really be work being done?*

Well, I think we all proved that point during COVID, didn't we? Or did these leaders experience some kind of amnesia? Or is it just selective amnesia because they have ulterior motives at play?

Cue the patriarchy. Think about who owns most of the office buildings and real estate companies that deal in commercial real estate. And why? Because they want to rationalize all of the money *they* spent on extravagant office spaces. Those with newly renovated lobbies complete with slabs upon slabs of nothing but white marble, I'm looking at you. We know that doesn't come cheap!

Or because they want to "get back to normal?"

Because "normal" was working *so well* for all of us! (Cue sarcasm.)

Except that it absolutely wasn't.

Here's the thing, we will never get back to that because "that," that ridiculous rat race called Corporate America, never did actually work for anyone who wasn't a white man, if everyone is truly being honest about it.

Hell, it didn't even work for some of the white guys doing it. Not underneath it all.

The return-to-office movement is just another mechanism of control, a mechanism that the patriarchy wants to continue to wield. It's another mechanism of white men trying to remain relevant. It's another mechanism of showing how illiterate most business leaders are to the true needs of their employees—and I mean all of their employees, no matter what their race, gender, religion, marital, or parental status, etc.

Clearly, the patriarchy doesn't care what you want to do, or what works for you and your family. They just want you in the damn office they spent so much ridiculous money on because if you don't go back, what will they do with the space? They'll be at a loss. So instead of them being at a loss, they want their employees to be at a loss—a loss of time, a loss of flexibility, a loss of autonomy.

So where does that leave us today?

We still have business leaders who are clueless to what their people need.

We still have knowledge workers who can do work from nearly anywhere.

But those two things seem to meet head-on in today's world, and they don't quite fit, much like a square peg in a round hole.

And then there is the math...and it doesn't add up.

Let's break it down to get a view of where we are today and what the future looks like in terms of the US workforce.

In the US alone, we lost around 1.1 million people from COVID-19[9]—and 1.2 million more people became disabled due to COVID-19 issues.[10]

Add to that the number of baby boomers retiring more and more quickly than they have in the past; we saw an increase of 3.2

---

[9] https://www.nytimes.com/interactive/2021/us/covid-cases.html

[10] https://www.americanprogress.org/article/covid-19-likely-resulted-in-1-2-million-more-disabled-people-by-the-end-of-2021-workplaces-and-policy-will-need-to-adapt/

million MORE baby boomers retire in the third quarter of 2020 than we had seen in previous years in the same quarter.[11]

Generation Z already has fewer people in the entire generation to fill the gap left by the retiring baby boomers, since the baby boomer generation was comprised of more than seventy-six million people and Generation Z is comprised of sixty-eight million people. And the next generation to retire after baby boomers is Generation X, which has about sixty-five million people.

Generation Z has also seen more entrepreneurs and side-hustlers than the baby boomer generation, so fewer of Gen Z will be in the workforce searching for open jobs. And then there are the members of Generation X and millennials who will need to leave the workforce partly or wholly to be caregivers for their baby boomer parents.

Where that leaves us is around 4.5 million fewer people in today's workforce than we anticipated.

In May 2023, the US Chamber of Commerce said there were 9.9 million job openings and only 5.8 million unemployed workers, so if every unemployed person in the country found a job, there would still be 4.2 million jobs without people to fill them.

What will that look like in one year? Two years? Five years? Ten years?

There's no getting around it, a Revolution of Work is due. Supply and demand elements of our labor market will dictate a change, and it needs to be a bigger and a more significant shift than we've seen over the last decade from the future-of-work people.

---

[11] https://www.pewresearch.org/fact-tank/2020/11/09/the-pace-of-boomer-retirements-has-accelerated-in-the-past-year/

If we continue to devalue humans and act like humans aren't the ones doing the working, more and more people will elect out of working for others. Unless we change that.

Supply and demand challenges are almost forcing our hands to do something about it. The Revolution of Work is here. And it isn't going anywhere.

Chapter 3

WHITE MEN—
THERE'S ROOM FOR YOU
HERE, BUT YOU MUST
BE AN ALLY

I was sitting on a bench, sobbing uncontrollably.

The sun was shining that day, but I remember specifically finding a bench that was in the shade because I didn't want anyone to see me crying.

What had happened to me, just five minutes prior, had probably happened to most women in the workforce at some point.

And what I kept telling myself is that even worse things had happened to far more people in the workplace.

I thought about getting in my car and driving home, leaving without a word to anyone of where I was going or what I was doing.

But I had a team counting on me.

I was part of the executive team for goodness' sake, and they needed me to keep on keeping on that day with a full work calendar ahead of us.

But as I had walked from the bathroom back to my desk, the CEO of the organization told me that he *really really* liked my dress, and then gave me a smile that made me uneasy and a gaze that went up and down my body like I was the steak on his dinner plate.

I stood there, frozen, not knowing what to say, and after he went back into his office, I hurriedly walked right past my desk and right out the office front door.

There was a rush of heat that swept up my neck and onto my face. If you or someone else you know has a similar reaction, it cannot be avoided, am I right? My face flushes when I'm enraged or shocked. Other people may flush with embarrassment. I knew at that moment my face was as red as a pepper, and I didn't need a mirror to confirm it.

But it had nothing on my rage inside.

In a comment that took him three seconds to say, he immediately made me question my attire, my abilities, and my worth. And I'm sure he wouldn't remember it if someone were to ask.

But I do. When I recall that memory, it takes me right back to that day.

This CEO had been an executive at one of the most well-known audio companies in the world.

And after sitting outside on that bench for about ten minutes, I wondered how many other women he had said similar, or worse, comments to, over the years. What other words or actions remained hidden behind large corporate doors?

I wish I could say that I marched right back in there to tell him a thing or two, or that I had a quick quip back at him when he so carelessly ogled me and made me feel uncomfortable, but I didn't.

It was still early in my career, and I didn't know what to do—like most who experience this.

But it's just one instance out of millions that happen every day to people around the world. In fact, nearly every woman I know has experienced some type of sexual harassment or assault at work.

Some of their experiences have been worse than others, but all of it is bad.

We can't keep allowing this toxic behavior to be allowed.

We can't keep allowing people to do these predatory things (and by the way, it's mostly white cis men doing this) and getting away with it.

We can't keep allowing these same men to headline conferences.

We can't keep allowing them to be in our industries at all!

They shouldn't have jobs. They shouldn't be allowed in positions of power, and they shouldn't be given passes when they are reported. Ever.

These predators should be in jail, without jobs, without compensation, without regard, without a thought because they gave no thought to those they have hurt, assaulted, and harassed. And if they have companies, I'm absolutely fine with them going bankrupt.

And if you are a white cis man protecting other white cis men in your industry, shame on you! You are equally as responsible because you are continuing to allow them to do horrific things to other humans. Your complacency is almost guaranteeing that they will hurt other humans. Think about that. Do you want that on your conscience?

We should never have to feel unsafe and be submitted to harassment and assault to do work. Never! Period. No one should have to choose between having a job and putting up with such remarks or not having a job. What kind of choice is that?

Work today still allows for these predators. Too often they are everywhere and involved in everything. That must stop.

Work is broken in so many ways, but in this way, it's actually dangerous.

If you are lucky enough to have never been assaulted or harassed at work, work is still broken for you. Toxicity and ridiculousness abound in the workplace environment, and it's time we change.

Before we dive into this next part, let me say this: again, I don't hate *all* men. There will be people who come for this book and will say that I hate white men, but what they are really saying is that they don't like that the power dynamic is shifting away from them being in charge and doing whatever they want, whenever they want. They want to hold the power so much that they are desperate to shock and distract.

However, it's abso-fucking-lutely going to be a chapter on hating men who hold up the patriarchy or are completely oblivious about their privilege.

But, if you are a white man, and you truly want to make a difference and stop being a white supremacist and male chauvinistic prick, then there is a place for you in the Revolution of Work. But, and let me make this very clear for you, society in the future will not be too wonderful for you if you are not an ally for others who look different from you.

So at this moment, I ask you to decide what type of human you want to be. Do you want to be one that only ever does things to serve himself? Or do you want to make a better workplace and a better world for those that don't look like, act like, think like, or come from the same background as you? If your answer is the latter, then you're on this journey with us, but we will need you to be active.

> White men want to hold the power so much that they are desperate to shock and distract.

There is a place for white men in this revolution, and it will likely take far more work than you've ever done to get in tune with yourself, your own privilege, and your own biases, and to be able to think about others, listen to others, and hold space for other perspectives and thoughts without getting defensive.

As you read this next section, please keep those ideals in mind. If you get mad or defensive, stop and assess why you might be feeling that way. Ask yourself, "Why am I feeling reactive to that statement?" or "Does this feel true to me?"

There are white men who are allies, who stand up and say, "No, that's not how we treat people," or "You can't say that to her," or even "She was speaking. Please [insert name here] continue before you were so rudely interrupted."

These allies are too few and far between, but they exist.

They may not get it right 100 percent of the time, but they do more than just try. They speak up and speak out. They go out of their way to make sure others who look and sound different have the space and platforms to elevate their voices. They work toward helping companies create equitable and inclusive workplaces that respect all humans. They listen to women and people in URGs when they talk, and they trust their expertise. They provide pathways and opportunities for people in URGs, not because they need to check a box but because they embrace and respect them.

One of the absolute best CEOs I've ever worked with is a white man. He was a first-time CEO, but he had decades of experience leading teams and working in some of the largest organizations in the world, many of which are household names. He brought in women to lead functions in his organization—for me, that was the People function—and he let us own our functions. He let experts be experts. He'd ask questions and listen to our answers, and trust that what we said was correct and that we knew the best path forward with respect to our departments.

This action may seem small to someone who hasn't been the only woman or person in a URG at the executive table, or for someone who hasn't been at the executive table yet in their career, but this is huge when it comes to the credibility, executive presence, and overall productivity of the company. He wasn't spending his days like so many first-time CEOs do—on the wrong things such as "so-and-so feels this way" or microman- aging every aspect of every function and trying to make every decision.

Spoiler alert: if you are a CEO, Founder, or COO, and you try to make every decision for your organization, you might as well give up now and let your entire executive team go because your company will not succeed in the long term. And your executive team will turn over constantly.

But this CEO also cared a whole hell of a lot.

He cared about people. He cared about getting things done and making an impact. Both things need to go hand in hand because focusing on just one will not work. When he asked a question, he listened actively and intently for the answer. And he stuck up for his team and his people. He even went to bat for them when it came to board of directors' meetings and investors' meetings. I witnessed it often. He is a man who truly deserves the title of leader and CEO.

But far too few white men do. It's unfortunate but true. Yet, they get handed millions of dollars without so much as ever having managed anyone before, let alone teams, and let alone entire businesses. (More on this in a later chapter.)

Holding up the patriarchy and holding up the status quo is dangerous. Yes, as a white man, it absolutely benefits you to do so, but it is harmful to those who don't look like you—deeply, deeply harmful. And I'd venture to say that if you were looking at this from a scale, you're doing two times, ten times, even one hundred times more harm to others than the good you are even doing for yourself.

But there are definitely selfish assholes out there. There are. There are white men, a lot of them, really, who only care about themselves or their own family. I mean, look at who was elected President of the US in 2016, and look at how many people voted for him. There is no lack of selfishness in our country.

I do think that some of you white men actually care about others. You do care about people who don't look like you. We just need more of you. There just aren't enough of you doing what it takes and going out of your way to make the lives of others who don't look like you better.

For those of us, including myself, who are white in this world, we have to look at our own privilege.

White men certainly have the most privilege in our country, but white heterosexual cisgender women have the next highest level of privilege. To read more about this, buy a copy of Regina Jackson and Saira Rao's book called *White Women: Everything You Already Know About Your Own Racism and How to Do Better*. As a matter of fact, go buy twenty-five or fifty, even one hundred copies, and give them to people you know. Then talk about it together.

We, as white people, must look at the privilege we have had throughout our careers.

And as white men, since you've had the most privilege, you've also had the most power. If you don't think there is a power play in work today, you're delusional, or it's just working so effortlessly for you that you don't even realize it exists. And that is what we call *privilege*.

Power dynamics where white men hold all the power is called a *patriarchy*. And that's why our world of work is so fucked up right now. Too many white men have held up a system that works for their benefit solely for the majority of the time, and we are now at the highest rate of employee stress. And we have the audacity to wonder why?

Come on, people. This isn't rocket science! (And I know rocket scientists. We have one in the family. They're smart!)

Power means authority, and in a work setting, authority discourages people from speaking up toward or against you. But to be fair, the authority brought to you and laid at your feet isn't really the authority that you yourself "earned" through hard work and struggles, no matter how much you all believe it is. And that same authority discourages people from saying anything that might go against the grain or against anything other than agreeing with you. Your power as white men exists because of the color of your skin, something that you have zero control over; you were born with it. Period. It was not your intelligence. It was not your hard work. It was not your education. It was not your natural abilities. Your power as white men is not based on anything having to do with anything *you* can control.

Your power exists because you are a specific color.

When you think about it, it's as absurd as my saying that the teal crayon in the pack has way more power because it's teal. *Like, what?* Who actually believes that the teal crayon has more power than the rest?

Full disclosure here: I know it is uncomfortable to think that your hard work didn't get you where you are right now if you are successful, but it is true. You think you "earned" this—and so do you white hetero cis women—but you didn't. The struggles and hard work you may have put in completely and utterly pale in comparison (pun intended!) to the mountains of struggles and seemingly insurmountable hard work and obstacles that those without white skin must endure just to get close to the income you have received and the titles you were given.

If you started in a middle-class family or at a higher income growing up in this country, you already have had opportunities other Americans have not.

If you woke up every day with one to two parents at home and did not go to school hungry, you have already had advantages other Americans have not.

Suffice it to say, there are thousands of things I could add here to show you how your life hasn't been as difficult and you haven't had to struggle as much as others may have had to.

Still thinking that you got where you are because you put in the hours and are just that smart, maybe even smarter, than most everyone else?

Think of it this way—if you are making a peanut butter and jelly sandwich, being white is like pulling the bread bag from the kitchen counter, grabbing a plate and knife that are both clean from the kitchen cabinets you own, spreading the peanut butter and jelly that you bought at the store, and smashing the two together. It may take you a whole three minutes to complete the sandwich and sit down on your couch to eat it.

Imagine you are making the exact same sandwich but you have obstacles and challenges that keep getting in your way—perhaps the bread is moldy, perhaps the peanut butter is expired, perhaps the electricity goes out and it's nighttime so you can't see and have no candles, perhaps you don't have a clean knife or plate, perhaps you have a screaming toddler who's yelling something about some superhero, perhaps you have to stop making the sandwich mid-way because you have to go and help your mom who lives with you go to the bathroom because she can't do so herself. All-in-all, the sandwich making takes thirty minutes.

Using this example as a metaphor for what white privilege looks like, it would take the white person ten times less time to make the sandwich with very little difficulty along the way. So while you think you "earned" your success, you honestly just didn't get in the way of it. And even if you did, you had fewer obstacles and challenges along the way to overcome than those who don't look like you. And it's likely you had a support system that allowed you to fail more often, and who provided you a safety net.

To stack on top of that, when you look at yourselves and think about hard work, I'll bet that many of you think only of other white people you know.

When you think of people at work, people at the grocery store, people at a restaurant, people in the world, you may default to whiteness. That's also an issue because the majority of the world is not white. So your default is centered on the societally made and (white) man-made premise that isn't even true.

The same thought goes toward patriarchy.

Studies have shown us that women are far better leaders, investors, and emotionally stable human beings, yet we continually get the opposite information or "studies" thrown in our faces. The numbers don't add up.

Centering whiteness doesn't inherently make you a bad human—it just allows you an opportunity to do better.

My hope is by shedding light on the rigid patriarchal system, you can see the ridiculousness that it is made up of and help you to be an ally and make change for others to be able to have the privileges you have enjoyed your entire life.

I hope we can all be allies and activists to change the world so we can create workplaces for all humans to thrive, not just white people and not just men.

But we need white men to change because you all do have the most power in our patriarchal society. If you help us and become allies, we can actually make real change. And if you don't, we won't. Because as Saira Rao and Regina Jackson have said in their book mentioned above—if you wanted to change the world, you would have already.

In order for us to make change, we first must agree that there is a problem.

And if you are paying attention, you'll see that the occurrences and trends I've experienced are not unique to me as a woman.

In fact, I don't know a woman, transgender person, or nonbinary person who works in a company anywhere out there who hasn't had something happen to them where they've felt disrespected or worse, by others in a work setting. And I know thousands of women, nonbinary folx, and transgender friends—some of whom have never even met me in person but have reached out with their own stories, just to make sure they aren't alone when they feel powerless, isolated, devalued, invisible, judged, and invalidated.

If you don't think this is a problem, think of this: How many men out there get together with other men and vent for hours with horrible stories about dealing with bosses, colleagues, or coworkers? Do you think insults, microaggressions, or blatant disrespect happen to them every day? Weekly? Monthly? Ever?

Because it happens to women and transgender and nonbinary folx all the time. For many, it happens daily, unless you have an ally as a boss and supporter.

So, white men, we need you.

We need you to stop going through life only thinking about yourself and your own family. Believe it or not, we get it that you love yourself and your family but remember that you cannot continue to carve out these slivers of privilege without it affecting those around you.

We need you to actually see other human beings and help them. Think about the people who work *for* you, including but not limited to the way you speak to anyone you are employing at any level. Do you approach them with the respect they deserve? Do you use the same tone you'd use with other executives at work? Because they are also equal to you. They are not less than, just because you employ them. They should be seen in the same way, no matter their level in the organization.

We need you to look outside of your own routine. Most people live inside of a bubble and go through their daily motions without seeing a lot. But what if we *decided* to open our eyes more and to actively help others more. What could we achieve and what good could we do in the world?

We need you to raise your head up above the clouds and see what's around you and who is around you. Or maybe just lower your head from above the clouds so that you can see how the patriarchy has put you sitting at the top of something that you never even helped construct but continually benefit from.

We need you to do active ally work to help us make this world better. Active allyship should be a continual and thoughtful presence of undoing past harm and continuing to make it easier for those that don't look like you to gain advantages in the world.

But white men aren't the only people we need.

If you are reading this as a white hetero cis woman, while we ask white men to help us with this change, we must also be the change for those people out there who aren't white.

Whether you believe it or not, the truth of the matter is that the world is currently set up to reward whiteness. Yes, to *reward* whiteness. That whiteness has allowed us—white women—to be the second most powerful players in businesses around the US.

And while our numbers aren't where they should be in board-rooms and executive offices around the country and the world, the numbers for other URGs are minuscule in comparison. The gaps are astonishing.

Let me ask you a question—who has the best ideas? Think of any great ideas you've read about or heard, or even have seen in the regular mainstream media—are they white? Or do you think of a white man because you've been predisposed to think of that stereotype? When someone is referring to thought leaders or high-paid C-suite leaders, who comes to mind? And why do you think that is?

The reality is that no human has all of the answers. No matter our skin color. But white people are continually given nearly all of the rewards as if we did.

That just doesn't make sense.

The same way that white men talk about meritocracy, we white women talk about "working hard" and getting where we are "despite everything we've had to go through," but again, "every-thing we have had to go through" is not even close to anything that others in URGs have had to deal with every day of their lives.

I've only had the lived experience of being a white hetero cis woman, and like many white hetero cis women, I used to think that I got where I was because I worked hard—until I started to actually think about how I got to where I was and what steps I took that were already at a higher level to jump from to be able to get to the next phase in my life or the next job. And those steps, I now realize, were built by the hard work of those before me who didn't look or think like me.

As a white hetero cis woman, I may not always have physical safety, especially at night or in getting to my car in a parking garage, but I have more physical safety than Black, Brown, Asian, and Indigenous folks have because of my skin color.

> The reality is that no human has all of the answers. No matter our skin color. But white people are continually given nearly all of the rewards as if we did.

I can wear a hoodie walking down the street without fear of being seen as a criminal and without fear of the police asking me questions and arresting me simply for walking down the street.

As a white hetero cis woman, I may not always get what I want and feel like I deserve, but that's the way it is for the majority of the time for other URGs. How many Black, Brown, Asian, Indigenous, disabled, and LGBTQIA+ people have done the work and not gotten the title, credit, or salary increase that should go along with it? Or that many of their white cis counterparts receive, even before starting down the path of actually doing the work?

> Those steps, I now realize, were built by the hard work of those before me who didn't look or think like me.

When we as white women walk into a room, unless the room is filled with all men—and especially white men—people listen to what we say. How often do you think Black, Brown, Asian, Indigenous, disabled, and LGBTQIA+ people feel heard every time they speak in business meetings? Or how many Black, Brown, Asian, Indigenous, disabled, and LGBTQIA+ people even feel like they can speak up or out at all at a business meeting?

I can breathe and live freely in this world as it is now for the majority of my life. This is the opposite of what it is like for other URGs.

So when I talk in this book about how white men can help women when it comes to dismantling the patriarchal workplace, I want you to think about how white women have to also be part of the dismantling of racism and ridiculously-set-up societal norms for everyone else.

And by not speaking up even for us in meetings when white men put us down, or tell us to "smile more, honey," or run a hand up our legs in a meeting when we didn't consent to that gesture— we are also doing a major disservice to every other woman out there, every other Black, Brown, Asian, and Indigenous woman, every transgender woman, every nonbinary person, and every person who doesn't want to be put in a box.

By staying silent and not speaking out for us and others, we are allowing this misogyny, sexism, racism, homophobia, and xeno-phobia to continue to exist—and not only to exist but to thrive. Our silence is just more fuel for society's fire to continue upholding the white patriarchy.

And to be fair, it's not only white men who put women down. We do it to ourselves and each other. And we have to stop that. We are not getting anywhere by fighting among ourselves.

> Our silence is just more fuel for society's fire to continue upholding the white patriarchy.

That's what they—white men— want us to do. They want us to continue to claw at each other so that we are so busy and distracted by each other that we have no time or brain space to deal with them. This way they can continue treating people badly, doing business badly, and probably all the while making more money because of it.

The mechanisms of control at least in the US are those where white men have the puppet strings. They are the marionette string-handlers, pushing us to distrust or dismiss each other so that they can continue to push forward and be more successful themselves.

White people, we need to do better. Even if you haven't had the full extent of privilege as other white people, you still have had loads more than those who don't look like you. I'm asking you all to do better. We don't deserve the rewards that have been given to us by society and that we have implemented to help only ourselves. And even the societal advantages we have had are still crushing when we look at it from a daily life stand-point, though not nearly as crushing for us as they are for those who don't have the same skin tone. The constant rat race, the constant hustling, the constant want and need to "be in the office" are all societal constructs that were put in place and we are perpetuating...for what? The norms of society and work aren't working for us either.

> They are the marionette string-handlers, pushing us to distrust or dismiss each other so that they can continue to push forward and be more successful themselves.

We are all burned out. We are all *over* work. We are all stressed. All of our health has been affected by work, some just more than others. So why do we keep doing the things that aren't working for us and sure as hell aren't working for those who don't look like us?

Why? Because it's known and comfortable? Does this make it right?

Shake off the comfort and the known. Let's work together to make something better, and to make something that works for all humans.

That's a work environment worth fighting for.

That's what the Revolution of Work is all about.

Chapter 9

WOMEN, NOW IS OUR TIME TO SPEAK UP AND OUT!

Imagine this...

You're sitting in a meeting where you are the only female in the room, and everyone in the room is white. It's a group of executives, and it's an executive meeting that happens every week to catch up on what is happening in the business. You are sitting there, hearing that the business you just joined is losing revenue and market share, and it needs to pivot to survive. After listening to where the company is, the financial status, elements at play, and opinions by nearly everyone in the room, you ask, "So, what are we going to do about it—what's the solution?"

Silence.

Two minutes pass.

You say, "Well, why don't we [insert amazing business idea here]?" The white men in the room scoff and say, "It will never work," so you remain quiet.

Twenty minutes later, after talking in circles, a white man replies, "I've got it—what about [repeats the same thing you said previously but in different words]."

And everyone at the table except you says, "Yeah! That's it! That's what we should do!"

Major eye-roll moment but something that happens all the time to people in URGs.

And after the disrespect, the gaslighting, and the stealing of ideas comes the quieting down. And then after, comes the feeling of being unsafe. All of which is in itself enough to create a toxic workplace, yet add them up, and you have what most people in URGs deal with in their careers at most companies.

In 2022, we saw the overturning of *Roe v. Wade*, the Supreme Court case that allowed for women to have legal rights to abortion and other reproductive rights. These were rights that we held onto as women as owners of our own bodies for nearly fifty years. The same rights that with the stripping of them showcased just how we continue to move back and forth in the same space of equality, not really moving far enough forward in women's rights and human rights across the spectrum for us to feel like those rights are safe.

With that news crushing most women in the US, the need to speak up and speak out became that much more necessary.

In my opinion, there is truly not a woman on this earth who believes she should *not* have rights over her own body. And for those who don't believe that—I truly believe that they just haven't yet tapped into their true inner selves to realize how not having rights over one's body is innately and supremely disconcerting.

But that's for another day and another book.

If we want something to change, we must drag the darkness that is the patriarchy and all of its inner workings, gender biases, harassment, toxicity, and sometimes maliciousness into the light.

The way that men have been treating women for thousands of years isn't new. It's so deeply rooted in our society in the US that it has become the default—much like whiteness is the default in the US. Neither is correct in any manner.

It was set up that way by white men to give the power to white men, and it is kept that way to keep the power with white men.

Every now and then, there is an illusion of power given up by white men, but it's only a glimpse of heavily woven hope where those same men pull that power back and pull the rug out from under us all—which is what we have seen with the overturn of *Roe v. Wade*.

But with the majority of buying power in the US belonging to women, and with more women in the US than men, we have the opportunity to make lasting change.[12]

But change doesn't come with silence. Change doesn't come with us sweeping yet another comment that was meant "as a joke" under the rug. Change doesn't come when we hide away in shame, like *we* did something wrong, when white men make horrific comments. We should be calling out the monstrosity publicly instead. Put away the pink pussy hats, and let's get loud where it matters.

We absolutely need to start standing up for one another at work. We need to stop saying things like, "I got here on my own, so they can, too" about other women—because to be fair, you never get there on your own, especially if you are a white person. Your privilege got you there. Without it, you wouldn't be where you are because you would have never had an elevated platform to jump from.

Silence is easy. It's easier to curl inside ourselves and constantly go over things in our minds. We as women tend to do that, wondering if we had said something or did something that seemingly allowed a man to treat us that way. We tend to look at ourselves and replay what we could have done or changed for a different outcome, but only once the situation is behind us.

Silence is also complacency. Silence allows for that same man to do that same thing to other women.

But we should be turning our efforts and words toward men, men who gaslight women and manipulate others, and especially those

---

[12] As of July 1, 2022, there were 165.28 million males and 168 million females living in the United States. https://www.statista.com/statistics/241495/us-population-by-sex/

who have done it for so long that they don't even know they are doing it anymore.

Merriam-Webster's Dictionary defines gaslighting as the "act or practice of grossly misleading someone especially for one's own advantage."[13]

Gaslighting happens all the time in the workplace. And sure, it doesn't *just* happen to us—anyone can gaslight anyone. But it sure happens far more to women and to those in URGs than it does white cis men.

And why is that? Control. Gaslighting is a way to gain and keep control. And when men can keep control, they can continue to hold up the patriarchy. And they remain at the top of the power sector.

"That's not how I meant it." "Your perception was off." "That's not how I took it." "You're blowing this out of proportion." "It's not that big of a deal." These are all examples of gaslighting.

If you have been out in the world and working for a little while, you'll have heard these phrases and probably shook your head a bit as you read them just now. These statements are also deflections. They truly say more about the person than they say about you. But none of these statements is okay. None of these statements should be said. And great leaders won't say them.

I have had no fewer than 1,000 women and nonbinary folx reach out to me over the past few years for support, empowerment, advice, or just honest-to-goodness conversation to make them feel less alone. And all of them were dealing with a form of one of the statements above coming from people and places of power in their organizations.

---

[13] https://www.merriam-webster.com/dictionary/gaslighting

Anessa Fike

Now, don't get me wrong. I will 100 percent answer the call of anyone needing some badass empowerment or turning the name calling of *bitch* to *bad bitch*, but this shouldn't be happening.

We are in 2024. And people are so intimidated by people having a voice. Why? Because it's not a white man's voice. But here's a little secret: What intimidates them more is when we join together en masse and use our collective and intersectional voices. It scares the status quo lovers shitless.

As I was listening to Meghan Markle's *Archetypes* podcast with guest Jameela Jamil, they spoke about women activism particularly being wrongly seen as "audacious." Like how dare we speak out and use our brains and our voices?!

Society has set up certain demographics to be *thoughtful, inspirational, and visionary* when they present ideas. But when women, nonbinary folx, and non-white men speak up and present ideas, tables turn, and people get defensive. Then they start the name calling—saying that they "are full of themselves," "overly confident," "boisterous," "boasting," "bragging," "speaking out of turn," etc.

In reality, it's the definition of a double standard. What breeds success for the white male demographic breeds contempt, jealousy, and otherness for those who aren't that.

Very early in my HR career, I thought I had figured it all out. I thought I found the perfect company with the most perks I had ever seen where I could get massages and pedicures every other week at work (yes, at work!). There was an entire game room, snacks were always available, and I could pick out cute items from Paper Source for my desk.

I spent years there.

I moved closer to the office—hell, I could even walk to work.

But as I kept getting promoted, I noticed that my voice was accepted less and less, and the ask for me to speak up and give my thoughts was dwindling. I noticed that in meetings, especially in meetings where I was the only female, I was told to sit down and listen more. One of my colleagues who had been at the company for years even told me once that I'd get farther if I just put my head down and worked hard, and that people would notice that more. And yes, she was a white woman. She should have done more and known better than to squash another woman like that. But she'd been so conditioned in society to say the thing that she thought was correct.

Looking back now, I know that was her own insecurity, sprinkled with jealousy as my own career progression quickly surpassed hers.

The advice she gave me was horrible. For women to have to be quiet to be accepted seems ridiculous. That we have to be mousy to make headway makes no sense. The idea that we can't possibly grow in our careers past a certain stage if we actually *use* our authentic voice and actually speak up for what we believe, like the men do, without fear of being regarded differently is preposterous.

Even so, none of that was what finally led me to leave.

It was the day that I realized two colleagues, one of which was an executive at the time and is still there to this day, played a horrible prank on me that went way too far. They gaslit me, and they made me question my own physical safety, which as women, we're often already questioning without added fuel to that fire.

I noticed something was off when I was recruiting for a person on my team. We often received hundreds of résumés for every role we posted, and I combed through them all, pulling out probably thirty to forty résumés of candidates to have phone calls with.

Now, if you know me at all or have worked with me in the past, you already know that those thirty to forty résumés were of people with different backgrounds, different experiences, different experience levels, and different writing styles, etc. There was a myriad of talent among that résumé group. And there was one résumé that was a bit interesting to me because it detailed an eerily similar background to my own. It stated that they had gone to the same university that I had, played the same sport I did there, and started out in recruiting as their foray into HR. Not entirely one in a million since I did go to university with more than 65,000 students every year, but something pushed me to take a call with this person because it didn't feel right.

I reached out via email to this person the same as I had done for those other thirty to forty candidates, asking them for a time that would work for them for a phone call. The person responded with an email matching their name, and I looked up their LinkedIn profile since it was listed on the résumé. Everything seemed legitimate, but there was still a very eerie feeling that I couldn't shake.

Once the person sent back the email with a time to connect, they kept diverting talking to me on the phone. They wanted to re-schedule a few times and had valid reasons. Ever the compassionate recruiter, even to this day, I'll reschedule if a candidate asks me to. We are all human after all.

But when I got on the phone with this person, the voice seemed muffled, like they were using voice-changing software, and the way this person answered questions was a bit off.

The person on the phone asked me questions about myself and my work, but not in a professional manner, more in a creepy manner. The hairs on the back of my neck stood up as I continued the phone call with this person, and when it ended, I felt a rush of uneasiness wash over me. This candidate seemed to be too close to my personal story, knew too many things about me that weren't exactly spot on but weren't at the level of a complete stranger, either. And the information they had was definitely more than I had put out on social media. I was fully aware of a sinking and vulnerable feeling, and my mind turned to wondering if I had a stalker.

As any female can tell you, this isn't an uncommon fear. We have to be careful walking alone at night, or walking to our car in parking garages that aren't full of people, or even running by ourselves. We are in constant awareness of where we are, who is around us, and especially when someone is following us too closely.

My mind wondered if this person was figuratively following me too closely. Or whether they were watching me walk to work every day. Or whether they were going to jump out at me from around a corner.

I felt unsafe. I felt worried. I felt uneasy. I felt out of control.

I went to work and tried to push through, and I kept going through the other candidate phone screens.

Then the person emailed me a day or two later asking for an update in the process—which also isn't uncommon—but seeing the email and the name immediately made the hairs on the back of my neck stand up again. I was sitting at my desk in the office, and my hands were clammy as I read the email. My heart was racing, and my brain went fuzzy all at once. I looked around the office, and something told me that someone was watching me. I could feel eyes on me. If you've never felt this way, count yourself lucky because it is not a good feeling.

I didn't have a stalker. I had colleagues who thought this all was the most hilarious thing that ever happened. They had planned and executed a cruel prank. And they had been watching me across the office when I opened emails, without my knowing this at the time, and had been laughing at my expense. All the while, they were oblivious to the fact that I was terrified. I'm sure my blood pressure was through the roof on those days, I barely ate, and I felt constantly paranoid and aware of everything. My husband told me that I should maybe take off and stay home until we could figure out what was happening. He was also deeply scared for my safety. But I, as most women do, said that my team needed me, and the candidates needed me, and I needed to continue to go to work.

Three days of agony later, a friend who was also a colleague asked me to grab a coffee. I didn't think anything of it since it was something we did often in that culture, walking to the coffee shop and talking and catching up.

After we grabbed coffee, she sat down on a bench outside of the office, and she told me there was something she had to tell me. She told me what she and the executive had been doing, that the résumé was made up, and that they were playing a prank on me together.

I stared blankly at her, not able to move. I was in shock.

I remember saying, "What?"

And she laughed and said that it was just a harmless joke. They thought it would be funny.

I was worried for my safety, my husband was worried for my safety, I was barely eating, my autoimmune system was shutting down because I wasn't feeding my body, and I was horribly stressed…and they were laughing.

"Harmless," she said.

Finally, after several minutes of silence, I was able to shake the shock. I told her how I was feeling, how I was worried for days before then, and how the entire thing made me feel horrible, vulnerable, and unsafe.

Her response?

"Oh, you're overreacting. It was just a joke!"

And when I pointed that out and asked how she would have felt if I had done that to her and pointed out that she was someone I thought was my friend, she told me not to be so sensitive.

What I didn't know then but learned later was that that day in the office when I read the email and looked around because I felt someone watching me, she and the C-suite executive were sending the email together, laughing, and waiting for me to respond. I'm glad they had so much time to play horrific pranks on people instead of benefiting employees by, I don't know, doing their own jobs?

This was the day I knew I couldn't stay at this "best place to work" because they had made my environment toxic. They had gaslit me. They had made me feel unsafe on my walk to and from work. They had made me feel unsafe while at work. They had made me physically sick with stress. And they did it all for a laugh, and not even a laugh *with* me, but a laugh *at* me.

Women can gaslight women just the same as men can gaslight women.

That day was also the day I lost a friend. I told her we were no longer friends because friends don't treat each other that way.

Still, I don't believe that either of them think what they did was wrong. I complained about it and reported it to the powers that be, but nothing was done. And they weren't even reprimanded in the slightest. They held high-level roles at the same organization for years. One of them is still there, leading people, if you can imagine. I can't even guess how many other people he has harmed by being in that position over the years.

I tell this story for one reason—if you have ever experienced something like this in the workplace, or something worse than this, you have every right to be pissed, enraged, mad, anxious, sad, and feel vulnerable. And your feelings are valid. And gaslighting is never ever okay.

I learned over time that their actions showed me who *they* truly were, what weaknesses and insecurities *they* had toward me, and their lack of ethical compass toward human decency.

It wasn't too long after that I started my own business and vowed to make it my mission to help companies create great workplaces for all humans so that people didn't have to suffer through pranks and other toxic mechanisms in work culture, just for a paycheck.

This horrific prank should never have happened. And if it did, then they should have been fired on the spot for making a colleague feel unsafe for no viable business reason, if it truly was a "best place to work." But guess what? They were also both white.

I wish that I would have had the courage at the time to put my story on LinkedIn and call out the company and the individuals. I also hope that in this Revolution of Work, we make safe spaces for people to exist, and that people like this who play silly pranks for no reason other than their own twisted amusement and/or to make themselves feel bigger or better are dragged into the light and never get executive titles again. They should never even manage people again. Ever. How can a person who does something like this lead any team or anyone well? By creating unsafe spaces? No thank you.

Sure, people make mistakes. We're all human. But malicious intent changes the mistake landscape, and there was absolute malicious intent to this.

Among the last words my former friend said to me were: "We just wanted to take you down a few pegs," because she thought I was being promoted too quickly.

Wow, some *friend*.

People like this can't be leaders in the Revolution of Work. Period. We have to demand better. We have to speak up and speak out. We can't let this toxic behavior continue.

And here's the thing, the game room I spoke about? There was no one ever in it. The massages that I had every other week? I had to have them almost out of necessity after this prank to calm my anxiety and stress levels from being in the same office as these people. And the "best place to work" award for this company? If you ask me, it should be thrown out the window. Great workplaces don't make you feel like this. Great leaders don't make you feel like this. No matter how hard I worked or how wonderful my work was, it didn't matter. This experience compounded my want and need to go out on a mission and make places better for all of us, which is why I'm writing this book today—to help make a change.

We shouldn't have to work in places that are like this, and business leaders should be called out for creating these toxic environments.

And allies need to actually be allies for each other—whether it's for another woman, a friend, a colleague, or a complete stranger.

Chapter 5

WHAT IS PROFESSIONALISM? STOP SAYING PROFESSIONAL WHEN WHAT YOU REALLY MEAN IS CONFORMITY

"Your tattoos aren't professional."

"Your hair isn't professional."

"Your outfit is distracting, and it's not professional."

My lived experience as a white woman is all that I've ever experienced, and I'm aware of all that privilege allows me and gives me in this world. And yes, even I have experienced being told I was "unprofessional" based on what I wore to work.

If you've ever been in Washington, DC, in the summertime, you know how sweltering walking outside can be—like you just walked into a sauna, fully clothed.

My place of work at the time didn't have a dress code. It was something that they touted and shouted to everyone who would listen. They said they trusted adults to be adults.

Makes sense in theory, but then you have adults who take it upon themselves to use their own biases to make comments and act on behalf of the company when they have no business doing so.

Like when a senior member of the People team pulled me aside and told me that my shorts were too short. Mind you, these shorts were nine-inch shorts. As a person who is 5'4," I don't have long legs to begin with, and these shorts were within a hand's difference from my knee. They would have even passed my high school dress code, which was decently conservative.

She went on to say, "Nobody thinks you are credible and won't respect you when you wear things like that."

As a people pleaser, this sent me into a mental tailspin. I questioned everything. I immediately went home, crying, and changed—and then went back to work until 7 p.m. that night. This conversation ruined my day and hindered my confidence in not only myself but also my abilities at work. *Could she be right?*

I started to think to myself all of the thoughts that run through so many women's minds early in their careers.

If I wear this, will I be considered serious enough but not too serious to be considered a bitch?

If I wear this, even though I like it, will I be looked at as too sexy?

If I wear this color, this shirt, this skirt... the list goes on and on.

Because in most corporate or business settings, what you wear tells a story. And as a young professional, you want your story to reflect the "right" you.

The older me knows better now.

The older me knows that what you choose to wear should be your decision, and any judgments against you are unimportant.

But all those years ago? Well, let's just say that I wore pants, mostly jeans, for the remainder of my time there, except for a few days here or there where I wore dresses that were below the knee.

In fact, my work uniform became jeans and a blazer. I was never going to let anyone tell me that my clothes made me less professional again.

Looking back now at the entire situation—in my logical mind, I get what was happening, and the shorts and the comments made by the woman had very little, if anything, to do with me. I was just who she was projecting her insecurities on at the moment.

I was ridiculed, shamed, and pulled aside based on one white woman's ridiculous thoughts on professionalism that she, and society, put on *her*.

And to further this point more, even my work uniform of jeans and a blazer later became a joke. After I left the organization, someone at this company dressed up as me for Halloween.

No, I'm not kidding.

> The older me knows that what you choose to wear should be your decision, and any judgments against you are unimportant.

This *I'm damned if I do, and I'm damned if I don't* type of bullshit is exactly what most people in URGs experience every day. (And by the way, the only ones who really aren't held to this standard? White men. Think about all the sweatshirts and jeans they wear. Is anyone questioning their professionalism?)

So for most women out there and for our nonbinary and transgender friends as well, it begs the question, how do we dress to not be "too sexy" or seen as "unprofessional"? It honestly seems like we can't win.

Still, it leads to the question: What does it mean to be professional? Truly?

Professional should describe someone who has a skill or knowledge base around a certain topic area, or the willingness to dive in and learn in order to perform the work at hand. Period. That's it.

And if we take that definition and apply it to most knowledge-based workforces today, then everyone is a professional. And it has nothing to do with the clothes someone wears, or the way they wear their hair, or the tattoos or piercings they decide with which to adorn their body.

Let's walk through the reasons people believe they can make such unfounded claims as to what is professional and what is not.

A white woman tells another white woman she can't wear shorts to work, even though there is no dress code. It was written in the employee handbook that there was no dress code. The same line of thinking allows people to think that a Black person's natural hair and an Indigenous person's tattoos are unprofessional.

It's actually all about control and insecurity. If a person can tell another person they aren't professional based on things that have absolutely nothing to do with the content in their brain and the intelligence they have, that person feels superior, and the other, the one who is being criticized and scrutinized then feels inferior.

Do we as adults actually believe that having blue hair makes someone less smart? Do we actually believe that having ink on skin makes someone less capable of doing their job? Do we actually believe that a suit and a tie make people's intelligence increase? Strands of protein and keratin, ink, and fabric—*these* are the dynamics of professionalism?

It seems so silly when you really break it down. It is what our patriarchal society would have us believe though.

Let's stop for a moment. I want you to close your eyes after you read this next sentence and really think about the answer for a few minutes.

When I say the word *professional*, what is the picture in your mind?

That picture tells me a lot about your values, or the values that you've bought into from what society told you to buy into. If the picture in your mind is a white man in a suit and tie carrying a briefcase, you have bought exactly the bill of goods that society wanted you to buy.

You, someone who you probably think of as a professional, bought that lie. Hook, line, and sinker.

Is a white man in a suit more capable than you are to do any job? Is he more intelligent? Does he problem solve better than you? Can he multitask better than you? Is he more strategic than you?

The answer is, "Hell no!"

Ryan Gosling looks great in a suit, but does it make him more intelligent? Ask Barbie.

It's just the perception that white men are or do these things better because our society is built upon whiteness as a default, and "professionalism" in that culture is based on white men in suits.

But who really needs to wear a suit?

Think about it, in most boardrooms across the country in Corporate America, do you see individuals with unique ideas with a myriad of alternatives in place that make them smart in business? Or do you see a sea of black suits, white shirts, and black ties in a room full of mostly one person's ideas and the other people agreeing with him?

But you, the *consummate professional,* are better than that.

You can finally see how thin the veil is that the patriarchy pulled over your eyes, and that *professional* means whatever we want it to mean.

A professional tattoo artist can make more than a CEO. A social media influencer can make more than a doctor. The successful owner of an empire of restaurants and James Beard Award nods can drive motorcycles and be covered in body art.

So now that you've seen the lie, you can see the truth: There is no consummate professional look.

There just isn't. There isn't one outfit or piece of attire that truly makes you a professional or not. Being a true professional is knowledge-based, it's problem-solving based, and it's skills-based. It's not a look you can buy off the shelf, no matter how many people tell us and no matter how many years they tell us we can.

And it absolutely is not reserved only for whiteness, white looks, and white people tendencies. That's called *control.*

The other side of this coin, though, is that people want you to think that there is *one* way to be a professional because it makes *them* feel better about themselves when they walk into the boardroom with a suit on. Hell, earlier in my career, even I thought that my future work life would be me, dressed in designer couture, while walking into a sophisticated NYC office building. But that's all just bullshit.

And by the way, I'm not hating on suits or blazers—I really adore them—but they are fashion, not the definition of *professionalism.*

They aren't suits of professionalism that magically absorbs into your skin and makes you great at your job.

The problem with professionalism is that it centers around whiteness and white men. It puts the patriarchy at the center, and again—hopefully you can see the trend by now—it puts the patriarchy in control of the power.

When people of the baby boomer era are asked what a CEO looks like, they will likely picture a white man.

> When I ask my son, who is a part of Generation Alpha, what a boss or a CEO looks like, he tells me, "You, Mama. You're a boss."

When people of the millennial era are asked what a CEO looks like, they may be split between several answers. I'm hopeful that when Generation Alpha is asked this question, their thoughts include a wide variety of answers.

When I ask my son, who is a part of Generation Alpha, what a boss or a CEO looks like, he tells me, "You, Mama. You're a boss." He is surrounded by friends of mine who are all female entrepreneurs and boss babes in their own right. He has also seen me build a successful business from home. He doesn't see me wear a suit and a tie or commute to an office every day.

The more CEOs, COOs, and people who look different from each other that we have at the executive table, the better off we will be in the world, and the better off businesses will be.

The deep secret about professionalism is that it's about control, and more importantly, it's about controlling others to keep them down and inferior to the patriarchy.

Professionalism is a way for those in power to look at people and easily keep them in a box. It is a mechanism that tries to put people into a limited scope in order to make them seem less human. Differences make humanity special. Humans are complicated and often unpredictable creatures with different thoughts, dreams, wants, and needs.

Patriarchal professionalism removes the myriad uniquities of humans and makes them conform to the mundane.

But it's all a ruse.

And don't get me started on the executives and leaders who love to use *professionalism* in performance reviews and performance appraisals.

> The next time you want to say *professional* or *professionalism*, drop in the word *control* or *conformity*, and see if it still feels good coming out of your mouth.

Actually, let's talk about this for a minute.

Patriarchal professionalism is based on one race's demographic of what a professional should look like. So when we talk about performance, is it really fair to use only one race's view for everyone else? And is it fair to squash everything amazing that they bring to the table?

Absolutely not!

The next time you want to say *professional* or *professionalism*, drop in the word *control* or *conformity*, and see if it still feels good coming out of your mouth.

Chapter 6

HR AND PEOPLE LEADERS, PART OF YOUR JOB IS TO PUSH BACK

It was my day off. Calendar blocked, out of office email on, and Slack turned off.

Yet, I had a people manager blowing up my phone.

I didn't answer the first few times. I thought, "Surely these executives can go without me for one day. Don't they know how to manage their teams?"

And then when the third call came through, I figured it was a really urgent and important issue at hand.

A manager of a large team was on the other end of the phone line. And when I swiped to answer the call, there were no pleasantries. It was, "I need to fire this person immediately."

My first question to this is always the same: "Tell me why you think you want to fire them."

He proceeded to tell me that the person had come off parental leave and was questioning their sales commissions while they were on leave.

And then I waited.

Was that it?

So, after a few moments of silence, I asked, "And?"

"And, how dare she think that we didn't give her the commission she deserves. I even went above and beyond for her during her maternity leave, and now she wants to act like I'm trying to pull the wool over her eyes?" said this manager.

My response was, "So, to clarify, she is asking you to double check that her commissions are correct from parental leave?"

"Yes!" The manager emphatically stated in an increased and enraged tone. "Can you believe her?"

"Was that all she asked?" I questioned.

"Yes, why?" the manager replied.

"What was it about her question that set you off? Did she approach it in an accusatory manner? Did she yell at you?" I asked the manager.

"No, I can't even believe she would question if we gave her the right commission while out on leave," he replied.

So I said, "Hold on one minute. Let me ping accounting really quick, and I'll call you right back."

I hung up the phone and sent a quick Slack message to accounting and asked them to pull her commission documents and payouts for the last several months. Understanding the commission structure, and quickly reviewing it on my phone, I found that the calculations were indeed off.

When I called the manager back, I said, "She's right to question her commission."

And he said, "No, she isn't! She is…[fill in things women commonly hear, such as aggressive, disrespectful, ungrateful, out to get me, questioning my authority, etc., because he called her about four names]. I don't believe a thing that comes out of her mouth."

I paused. I asked the manager to take a breath, and then I said, "I need you to take a few minutes and listen to me, and I have some feedback for you. Are you okay with that?"

The manager said, "Sure."

And over the next hour conversation, I walked him through how dangerous assumptions are, how we were not going to fire her, how she was correct to question her commission check because it was incorrect and set forward a plan to make sure he didn't hold inappropriate and different expectations over her because she had come back from maternity leave.

I pushed back.

This is what real, true HR, People, and Talent leaders do. It is part of the job.

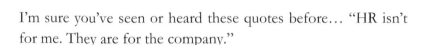

I'm sure you've seen or heard these quotes before… "HR isn't for me. They are for the company."

"You can't trust HR."

"HR won't help you."

And for some HR (human resources) departments out there, this is very true. HR has gotten a bad reputation because the actions of those in HR departments haven't always been great.

The HR departments I'm talking about that give the rest of us bad names are the ones that…

…pay attention to only compliance, risk, and paperwork.

…think that squeaky wheels are bad.

…don't address trends or problems.

…don't speak up toward or push back against leaders behaving badly.

…allow toxic employees to stay and cause further trauma.

…create policies for only a few employees because they want to make sure they CYA. (Cover your ass—for those unfamiliar with the acronym.)

…are in the profession for control, not to help people. (We see this often in other industries as well.)

…are made up of all or mostly white people.

…don't decouple performance and compensation.

…don't believe in the justice or equity part of DEIJ, IDEA, or DEIB (D= diversity or disability, E= equity, I= inclusivity, J= justice, A= accessibility, B= belonging).

…are not looking proactively into the future and only reacting to fires that need to be put out.

…are fine with the status quo.

Trust me, I can say this because I'm part of the industry—I have seen some horrible HR teams.

But there is hope.

There is a new wave of HR professionals who no longer want to be associated with HR and human resources, and rightly so.

Nearly fifteen years ago, HR started to move toward People Operations, or Culture, or Talent Operations.

The new People leaders were looking to figure out how to adapt to changing business dynamics, figuring out how to add to the bottom line instead of constantly draining it.

And guess what? Adding to the bottom line means treating people better, and the better you treat people, the better your bottom line looks. It's not just good business; it's good humanity.

As someone who has been in the industry for almost as long as mentioned above, there has been constant change in the field. People leaders now have about 150+ items on their list of what they are in charge of, and in some orgs, that even means IT, internal communications, executive coaching, and finance. Post-2019, People leaders have added even more to their plates, including pandemic-related items, mental health, and overall employee well-being. HR, People, and Talent is not the same as it was pre-COVID, and it likely will never be again.

But here's the thing that most aren't doing enough about: actively changing work by being vocal about it. They aren't pushing back. They are going along to get along, and that is dangerous.

I think the lack of vocalization of People leaders stems from the fact that historically, HR has been a tight-lipped, confidentially engrained department, and most are afraid of saying something they shouldn't. For years, there has been this invisible, never-stated rule that HR people shouldn't ever say how they really feel, shouldn't say anything negative about the company, should always be the company cheerleaders, and should also be the ones who solve the problems, whether behind the scenes or as the figureheads for any hard information that the executive team needs to communicate to the organization.

Therein lies the problem because HR and People are also employees, yet they aren't treated as such, and they tend to have to mediate between two sides, feeling constantly stuck in the middle.

But it is absolutely imperative that People leaders speak up and speak out when their leaders aren't doing what they should, to push back on the same leaders when they are making bad choices for their people, and to call out biases, racism, xenophobia, homophobia, transphobia, etc., when they see it, every time they see it. Every. Time.

Now, I get it. This is tough. The pushing back is tough. The speaking up is tough. It's hard.

And as People leaders, we have so much on our plates, so keeping it all up in the air is tough and hard enough as it is. But we have to. We are the human leaders in the org.

Repeating—we are human leaders—not just white human leaders.

But too often, People leaders don't protect, uplift, help, and promote all humans in the org.

Why? Because it's tough. It's hard. See a trend here?

But I'm going to say this—if you can't do the tough and the hard, you absolutely should not be in People leadership. At all. Ever. Period.

If you have a problem with speaking up, speaking out, pushing back, or having confrontations and tough conversations, get out now because without doing these things, you are not doing your job. And by not doing your job fully, you are doing a disservice to your organization and the people in it.

We as human leaders have a responsibility to uplift humans in the org and bring equity to our organizations.

Equity does not mean paying everyone the same for every job—it means paying the women, nonbinary folx, transgender friends, disabled, Black, Brown, Asian, and Indigenous people more because they have systematically and socially been undervalued and underpaid for probably their entire lives.

Equity does not mean creating blanket policies. It means creating policies that work for people to be respected and valued at work and creating policies that give people enough room for empathy and to breathe—yourself included. Policies are meant to create guardrails and guidelines for how things happen and flow in your organization. Policies are meant to be used as starting points that then can change as your culture does.

As a People leader—as a human leader—you are responsible for being the eyes, ears, and mouths of people not in the room. You are the representative of each and every person in your organization, especially the ones who continually get looked over.

So when you sit in a meeting, and you allow words to be spoken, without admonishment or objection, that are a hindrance to employees, you are now an accomplice to those words.

You are not saved because you said nothing. You are not saved because you let someone be themselves in all of their toxic glory.

You, as a People leader, are held to a higher standard. You have to be because you are in charge of humans.

And as a profession, we have a long way to go.

I've been one of the very few people who I've seen in my career (and this even goes back to when I was first starting out in the late 2000s) who spoke up and spoke out, even with colleagues and executives.

> When you sit in a meeting, and you allow words to be spoken, without admonishment or objection, that are a hindrance to employees, you are now an accomplice to those words.

There may be one or two people who join me in an organization and who feel compelled enough to speak up and out, but the majority of people just go about their days without trying to change anything. And for some of you, the white ones in the audience reading this, you have the luxury of doing that. Your counterparts who don't look like you don't have that luxury.

To be very honest with you, both then and now, I didn't and don't care about what it meant and means for me when I speak up and speak out, as long as I was able to make the workplace better for others who don't look like me.

And is it tough? Absolutely! Is it grueling and exhausting? Hell yeah it is. But can I look myself in the mirror and say that I've never kept silent when I shouldn't have? Absolutely. As a People leader, can you say the same?

We have an opportunity right here and right now to be the changemakers in our organizations. And if you aren't ready or don't know how, you either need to figure it out or bow out. These organizations aren't going to change without us, so it's either they stay the same or *we* try to change them.

I don't know about you, but I feel far better about myself thinking that I tried as opposed to giving up without an ounce of fight.

As People leaders, we must lead by example first and foremost. We must establish trust by not promising things we can't deliver. We must support and actually push for transparency across organizations. We must let our teams know we have their backs, and after we've shown that to be true, they will *feel* it. We must let our teams know that if they mess up, we take the blame. We must not only be advocates for the organization as a whole, but we must also remember that our own teams are a part of the organization, and also employees, and that we need to push equally for them to ensure they have the resources and support they need. We must make it okay for people to fail and learn from their mistakes. We must praise in public and teach in private, unless of course the person we are praising prefers to be praised in private. We must tell our teams that we ourselves don't have all the answers. We must not silo our organization. We must not have toxic positivity and act like we have got it all together. We must be human. We must be vulnerable. We must be honest. We must be courageous. And as People leaders, we must push for change.

There is no perfect organization. There is no perfect company. And even though there are companies out there that will tell you that they are perfect, the perfect company doesn't exist. It doesn't exist because companies are made up of people, and people are fallible.

We have flaws, all of us. But we have to push to be better and create spaces where people don't need to wear professional masks to show up at work. We have to work toward creating environments where people feel seen, heard, and respected—as well as paid fairly and according to their whole life experiences and skill sets, not just what titles they've been given, degrees they have earned, or letters that they have after their names.

Culture, DEIJ, DEIB, and IDEA are not all on us as People leaders, but we do have a heavy responsibility and burden to help them move forward. And if those things aren't important for us, it gives leaders of other departments the excuse to not have it be important to them.

I'd like to think that most of us got into the People and Talent fields to help people, to do good work for a better tomorrow, and to help others feel safe and heard. If you don't push for change, you aren't doing what you got into the industry to do.

I've also witnessed too many People and Talent leaders take on too much. Don't be afraid to ask for help. Don't be afraid to pull in consultants where you lack a skill set yourself or it is lacking in the company. Don't be afraid to pull in fractional help when you need to get a project done that keeps getting pushed to the back burner.

And don't be afraid to talk through your own biases—we as humans all have them. By being aware and constantly working on your own biases, you can do more good than harm. In order to truly see others and see what makes them beautiful and special, we have to be able to get past the barriers we have put up in our minds for whatever reason. For most people, biases are ones we have learned growing up. You will often hear that children aren't biased, and it's true because it is a learned trait. As we go through life, our brains find paths to least resistance, and for some, those paths become biases toward or against some things or groups of people. From the words our parents and friends speak, to the things we see in entertainment, to the way certain groups of historical peoples are talked about in school (or a lack thereof in most cases), we establish biases almost as layers of the onion over time. And I'm asking you to start to pull those back.

And don't spend your days just putting out fires because the fires, though they are urgent, are taking time away from your doing the work that is most important: changing the work landscape for all humans.

We must push back against the societal norms put into place by the patriarchy. We must push back against leaders that think people in URGs don't know as much as they do.

We must push back on people in the organization that think control mechanisms equal good people practices.

Because none of these mechanisms are actually successful in creating better work environments like the patriarchy would have you believe they are. They only exist to continue to allow the patriarchy to stay in control.

Chapter 7

FUNDING AND COMPANY BACKING

It was the time of year in Washington, DC, when rain and snow creates a gray and white slush around the city.

My husband—he works in the business with me—and I were setting out to meet a new client at their office space.

When we were greeted at the entrance to the office space, we were shown where the coffee and snacks were (if you have worked in start-ups before, you know these things are par for the course but set up to show the illusion of a great place to work) and led to a small conference room where the executives sat.

Previous to this meeting and even before signing the contract, I personally walked through our core values as a business with the CEO and COO. I told them both exactly what we were about, how we would go about working with them, and what we'd expect from them. They agreed.

As we started to settle into the conference room, the CEO popped his head in to say hello and asked if we wanted coffee. We both nodded, and the CEO asked one of the other employees to grab us each a cup. I told him that we could grab it ourselves since we were shown where it was when we came in. The employee looked at me and smiled, and I could see her release tension in her shoulders when I said we could get the coffee ourselves.

(I thought nothing of those brief few moments until later.)

When we were getting settled, the CEO shook my husband's hand, but didn't shake mine. I didn't think anything of it since I was around the other side of the table. The COO shook both of our hands.

Coffee in hand, we sat down with the CEO and COO and started into the questions we normally ask when we are getting to know a new company and its culture for the first time. We spend time learning and asking questions so that we have a good foundation and knowledge base to work from.

We started around 9 a.m., and by 9:10, I could tell something was off.

When we ask questions of our clients, we expect them to tell us about the people in their org, the way that they themselves feel about the culture, the way people interact, any challenges they are having, any wins they've recently had, and any projects or deadlines they have coming up as an organization that we should know about. Sometimes that's new funding; sometimes that's a general reorganization, which doesn't always mean layoff, it could just mean that the company has grown to a size where they need to then rightsize their organizational structure and titles. And sometimes, especially over the last few years, they tell us about layoffs.

But when we asked this CEO a question, he went into long monologues about the philosophy of everything from how human beings act in the world to, and I'm not even kidding you, why we as humans are even on this planet. His answers really had little to do with the culture and the question at hand. I realized pretty quickly that this man loved to hear himself talk and didn't love to share the spotlight, no matter how small the conference room was.

After an hour of meeting with him, I became super aware that he never looked at me during his whole soliloquy about the philosophical ways people are on this earth. My husband noticed it, too.

So nearly an hour later, my husband finally reached his limit. This CEO had asked him a question about our consulting firm, and my husband then said, "You'll have to ask Anessa. She is the CEO. She can speak for herself."

The only thing I can think that this CEO experienced at that moment was true disbelief and bewilderment. He paused, not looking at me, cleared his throat, and then almost as if it was the most painful thing he could do, he swallowed and looked me in the eyes for the *very* first time the entire morning.

He then asked the question again, and I responded.

What came to fruition over the two weeks of working with this client was that his behavior in our initial meeting was not an anomaly. It was not a one-off nervousness in working with a consulting firm to help make his culture better (and trust me, he'd absolutely never actually admit to anyone publicly that his culture was in trouble in the first place—his advisers and investors had told him that he needed help, so it was more of a forced consulting engagement on his part). He always spoke to my husband on virtual meetings the same way that he did in person, and the meetings happened the same way, as if I wasn't even in the room.

It was almost like he said to me, "Go home, honey. The men have got this. We don't need any little women around these parts."

But of course he didn't say that, not blatantly or to my face anyway. He did it in a much more nuanced way because isn't that always how these things go? They are nuanced and not blatant, until they are, so that these men (and yes, he is a white man) can maintain plausible deniability, at least in their minds.

After doing more research on the company over the week after that initial in-person meeting, I came to find that no woman had lasted at the company for more than nine months. No woman, at all, *none* since their founding. Only men could last more than nine months at this company.

The reason became absurdly obvious the more we talked to the executive team and the more we talked to employees internally. It was known throughout the organization that the CEO was a ridiculous sexist. It was also known that if the company made it big, their equity could be worth a pretty penny, but still, women at some point (before nine months) realized their mental health and well-being were worth more *now* than the possibility of money in the bank later.

There was even a small group of women in the company who got together to talk about how awful this CEO was, and they tried to broach the subject with him numerous times.

Want to know what his solution was before we entered the conversation?

He thought that bringing together a group of employees who wanted to improve culture *with him* being at the helm and leading the discussions would work. Talk about the perpetrator triggering those who he has done disservices to!

And in those discussions with that group, he said everything was going great! He said that no one had voiced any issues to him.

So during our first few weeks together, we talked to him many times in various ways, asking if he'd step away from leading that group, even for just a few months, to see what came out of it. To see, if perhaps, the people in that group weren't entirely comfortable with speaking up when he was in the same room. He said we were preposterous, and he said that he knew his employees. "They don't want that," he said.

After two weeks, it was very clear that this company was in chaos with its culture, bleeding woman talent for no other reason than its CEO, and yet, he wasn't interested in changing a thing. We even asked him whether he anticipated changing anything when he brought us on to help, and he said, "No, it was really just to check a box."

I called him shortly after that to tell him that we were firing them as a client.

If a CEO is a sexist asshole, we can work with them if and only if they are willing to change, even slightly. But this CEO was not. He was only interested in his own thoughts, his own words, and his own very skewed scope of what a great culture is. Oh, and by the way, he frequently said that he was much smarter than anyone else in the organization.

I can't say all of the names and words he called me during that client breakup call. He was belligerent as he screamed at me and basically threw around every name that men yell at women—*at me!* I remained calm and collected. But you know, side note, women are the ones who are so emotional and hysterical, right?! Insert frustrating eye roll for the double standard here.

He told me that he spoke to people about me prior to bringing me on and knew that I was a direct bitch (which, to be fair, I am sometimes when people need to hear things they aren't hearing), but he said that he figured he could just work with my husband and ignore me so that it wouldn't be an issue.

Wow. The audacity of people, right?!

In this rant that went on for forty-five minutes, which was mostly him talking and me remaining silent after the initial, "This isn't working out, and we need to conclude our relationship based on your words and actions," he even said to me that he had a woman as an executive coach and that *that* should be worth something.

My response to that was, "Do you actually listen to her and apply what she says?"

His answer was silence, and it told me all I needed to know and confirmed that us firing them was the absolute right decision.

I had friends work for this same organization months and years after we fired them, and after the first week, they called me and said, "Get me the hell out of here."

To this day, I've had countless women from there reach out to me to find confirmation that the workplace culture was as jacked up as they had thought it was—not because I reached out to them, but because word got around that I was a safe space for people from there to talk through their experiences. They said they felt gaslit, stupid, and isolated during their time there.

But here's where things get interesting, because, let's face it, leaders sometimes suck (more on this later). Some of the investors of this company are people I know. These investors tout working with companies that treat employees well, but if they spent more than sixty minutes with this CEO, they would have seen that this was not the case.

Yet, they invested millions of dollars in this white man who'd told us himself that he had only one failed and singular leadership experience before that. Even one iota of research would have told them everything they needed to know—and would still shred the vote of confidence that their supporters trust in them now—which is to help fund companies that treat people well.

There are two lessons here:

1) If you know in your soul and deep in your intuition that someone isn't respectful of you, that someone deeply hates you simply for your gender or your skin or any other piece of you that is you, or that someone who has a trend of treating people like you poorly over and over again, you are likely not alone, and you absolutely should not feel isolated. Seek out people who may have experienced the same thing. Because here is the deal: those types of people thrive on secrecy because it helps them maintain their power, just like the patriarchy. It's also typically why you find that so many white men act like this—because they feel like they have the full support of the patriarchy, and they sort of do until we change it. Strip them of some of their power by using your voice to speak out, or by using your feet to remove yourself from the company.

2) Investors put money into start-ups and smaller organizations to make money. Period. There is no other reason. Now, there are some (very few) investment firms owned and operated by women and URGs, but there aren't enough of those yet. The majority of investment firms (private equity (PE), venture capital (VC), Angel, etc.) are owned by white men, and what do white men like more

than power? Money. They don't care that the CEO of one of their portfolio companies is a complete and utter asshat. They care about him making them money. I've searched and searched for other reasons—trust me, we've worked with enough start-ups, VCs, PEs, etc., to know that at the end of the day, they truly just want to see those dollars stack up. Because if they cared about the people in the organization or how those people are being treated, they absolutely would stop giving so many white men with no experience millions and millions of dollars, and they'd start funding leaders who actually have EQ (emotional intelligence) and the experience to treat people well *and* lead a successful business (i.e., the millions of women, disabled, LGBTQIA+, Black, Brown, Asian, and Indigenous people who have amazing ideas and experiences).

I know, I know, you're probably saying, that is really depressing, Anessa, so how do we fix it?

Well, the answer is layered and complicated, but not impossible.

Investors really need to start digging into *who* they are investing in as much as *what* they are investing in.

I've had experience after experience with CEOs who have raised money from investors that I knew, but after spending one afternoon with them and asking them questions about their culture, I realized the CEOs were far from the "great leaders" they so proclaimed to be.

Potential investors should do their due diligence about how a leader treats their people. Honestly, even doing ten minutes of research on LinkedIn can tell you a lot about the person leading the company you want to invest in.

Many CEOs aren't held accountable for how they treat people. All people. They may be accountable for where the money goes and can track that easily, but do they track their interactions with their most important assets?

To get rid of the bad behavior that many CEOs—and others— exhibit, we have to make sure that when white men do bad things, we hold them accountable. And if a white man doesn't have the experience to run a company, then don't give him millions of dollars. Sure, you can give them a chance every now and then but start small. Start with the money that most investors give women, disabled, LGBTQIA+, Black, Brown, Asian, and Indigenous people, and then have them show their success before you give them more. Seems only fair, right?

I hear you; the accountability-for-white-men thing is super hard because they still hold the power in a patriarchal society.

As a society, we've been trying and failing to do this for centuries. White men have been the default for the breadth of history in the United States. We have been led to believe that white men make the best leaders. Refer to any history book in American schools, and you will find that the white men are exalted, and others are barely if ever mentioned. What we are now realizing is that those books are (or were) also published by white men (or by companies with white cis hetero men as owners). But why do we have to keep repeating the same problems before we start to learn? Or before we start to fix it? We keep putting the same kind of people in leadership positions and then we wonder why nothing changes, and, in fact, we often find it actually gets worse.

Do we have to keep pumping millions and billions of dollars into these organizations that have people pee in soda bottles instead of treating them like humans and giving them breaks? Or can we create a new way of working where people feel seen, respected, heard, challenged, and fairly compensated, and the company makes more money because of that?

It baffles me just how many people have experienced the disrespect and ineffectiveness from just one CEO's leadership, and yet, he still got millions funneled to him, some of it coming from another very well-known, white-male-centered but highly respected, world-renowned investment firm. Why? How can this keep happening?

It happens because those investment firms themselves truly don't treat people well, not at the core. They "treat people well" by paying them tons of money for their silence. So people deal with the throes of mental health wars and feeling inhumane because the money is so good. I get it—I don't fault those people.

I fault the people at the top who set up their culture this way. It wouldn't stand if they didn't stand for it.

Funders keep giving founders millions of dollars without assessing the quality of the leadership team or the company's treatment of and value of their human capital. And to be honest, if you look at most companies today, especially tech companies, most of the company is built on knowledge, intellectual property, and human capital, and they are valued with that in mind—the business is valued based on intangible assets. (On the opposite side, most manufacturing, logistics, and agriculture industries that rely on manual labor and physical work have more tangible goods and inventory that are core to the asset column in their businesses; and therefore, their businesses are valued based on the tangible assets.)

Yet, even with the majority of a knowledge business's valuation being based on the humans in it and their expertise, this cycle keeps happening. But should it? How do we change it? How do *you* change it?

Well, first and foremost, you speak up. You use your voice. You stop quieting that intuitive voice inside you, and you scream it out when you see a trend that supports the patriarchy, the trend that excludes anyone who isn't a member of the white boys' club, happening in your workplace.

Second, venture capital, private equity, angel investors, and other investing sources need to seriously start taking the humans in the businesses they are buying and managing—and giving capital to—seriously. They need to do actual due diligence in more than just finances and assets. They need to go beyond spreadsheets and business plans, margins, and ROIs (returns on investment). They need to meet more people and gather actual day-to-day experiences from more employees in the organization who report to the CEO, founders, or executive team. I've been saying this for years and years. And now, firms are finally starting to tiptoe down this path.

> I fault the people at the top who set up their culture this way. It wouldn't stand if they didn't stand for it.

Bryan Smith and Ketan Seetha have a company called LEON VC[14] that is helping investors with gauging and assessing not only human capital value but also founder (and executive leadership) potential.

Human capital and executive leadership are huge dynamics and indicators to whether a company is successful or not—both in the short and long terms—especially with more and more people in younger generations committing to dealing with less and less crap from work and leaders.

Think about it: if you have a start-up that has been funded with $50 million but the leadership team is made up of a bunch of white men who also happen to act like assholes, then:

1) your talent acquisition efforts are going to be harder because you lack a diverse team, which showcases to most people you don't prioritize diversity, equity, inclusion, and justice internally; and,

2) your employee retention will go down, leading to your talent acquisition and recruiting costs going up.

Where that leads at the end of the day is to a company that may be losing more money than it is getting in revenue, simply be-

---

[14] https://www.leonvc.com/

cause the leadership team lacks emotional intelligence and likely (because I've seen it too many times for it not to hold truth) self-awareness.

People often—especially journalists, i.e., my former self—tell you to follow the money. If you follow the money of work, culture, and leadership, most roads point to white funders funding more white founders, which then produces more jobs for predominantly white people.

In fact, white founders typically receive some $35 million more across the funding cycle than Black and Brown founders.[15]

And in 2023, the numbers looked even worse for founders who were not white. Crunchbase released information in early 2024 that confirmed what a lot of people thought was happening; Black founders were receiving even less funding than their white counter-parts. Funding for Black founders has declined since 2020, with the amount of funding allocated to them hovering around 1 percent in 2021 and 2022; but then in 2023, the percentage of funding dropped even more to 0.48 percent, or $661 million out of $136 billion.[16]

> If you follow the money of work, culture, and leadership, most roads point to white funders funding more white founders, which then produces more jobs for predominantly white people.

Economically, this leads to white people gaining more and more wealth, and the rest of the human race seeing the wealth gap (and the job and career gaps) widen.

---

[15] https://fortune.com/2023/03/06/white-founders-receive-more-funding-black-and-brown-founders/

[16] https://techcrunch.com/2024/01/17/funding-black-founders-down-in-2023/

It just doesn't make sense. Great ideas and innovations are not just limited to the minds of white people. And while we are on the subject, great ideas and innovations are not just limited to the ex-FAANG's (Meta, formerly Facebook; Amazon; Apple; Netflix; and Alphabet, formerly Google) of the world or those who graduate with Ivy League degrees. Those are typically just the ones who have experienced the most privilege.

> Economically, this leads to white people gaining more and more wealth, and the rest of the human race seeing the wealth gap (and the job and career gaps) widen.

We all must do better. Every part of the ecosystem of a company and a business has to do better.

I can't think that anyone who *truly* wants to better society only wants white men to succeed, but if you look at the funding statistics and listen to what the patriarchy tells you, it sure seems that way.

Chapter 8

MOST FIRST-TIME FOUNDER CEOS REALLY SUCK

(Yeah, they do.)

If you've ever worked at a start-up with a first-time founder who is also the CEO (or if this first-time founder CEO is you), reading this chapter may have some triggers for you. Fair warning.

If you haven't yet had this unique experience, you're in for a bit of a pulling back of the curtain when you see how most first-time founders who give themselves the CEO title actually work.

Let me preface this chapter by saying that not all first-time founders are like the following stories, but in my experience of working with nearly one hundred first-time founders, these stories and experiences are 99 percent the way first-time founders work. And thousands and thousands of my friends and colleagues in People and Talent share my feelings about this and commiserate.

Some people love working with first-time founder CEOs. Some people embrace the challenge. Others hate it, despise it, and never return to it.

For me, I'm one of the former. I thrive in the type of challenging environment where first-time founders are learning how to manage people for the first time, managing their own emotions and emotional intelligence, managing their companies, managing new funding, and managing their board of directors—because I'm able to both act as chief people officer and executive coach to them.

In fact, there are many first-time founders of tech companies who have done very well (many who are household names) that I've been able to be an executive coach for over the years, confidentially of course.

But there are some who just really struggle to get out of their own way. They struggle with allowing others to help them to grow and expand their "baby" because it all started with *their* idea and the fact that they started something from scratch.

First-time founders mostly start out with a disruptive idea for a company that will do something better or different from what the industry has been doing for years and years.

They truly believe that by having this idea, they must be smart enough to learn everything else needed to run a successful company, and many of them also believe they can achieve unicorn status easily. (Oh, and by the way, most of these first-time founders who we have worked with are, yes, you guessed it, white men. Founders in general—as polled in 2019—are 77 percent white.)[17]

And so, if you've ever wondered what's up with all of these tech companies treating people badly, not understanding how to do business well, or having a seemingly large number of layoffs, you can also tie it back to the last chapter around the patriarchy supporting the patriarchy through funding. They come from privilege, and that privilege connects them with others of the patriarchy and *voila*! They have start-up money.

(Starting to see the trend with what's so wrong with workplaces now?)

When you become a founder, you almost need to be a little egotistical. You need to also be pretty optimistic. You need to have a lot of confidence in not only yourself but your idea because you are the one pushing it forward from first thought to development. You need to be all of these things because starting a business is hard, it takes a lot of hard work, it takes a lot of hours, and it takes a lot of overcoming rejections, resistance, and naysayers.

I honestly get it—to an extent. Founders have to have increased levels of confidence because for some, that confidence is all that is keeping the new start-up alive, almost by brute force. Founders

---

[17] https://news.crunchbase.com/venture/untapped-opportunity-minority-founders-still-being-overlooked/

have to also have the hope and knowledge that they will succeed, even when all roads point to them *not* succeeding.

There is even a term for this, one that I'm pretty sure is not scientific but one you'll find all over the internet and in start-up spaces, called "Founderitis." It can also be called "Founder's Syndrome."

If you search Founder's Syndrome, you'll find little on it outside of tech industry jargon, but I did come across this particular definition (and the descriptions that follow) on Wikipedia: "the difficulty faced by organizations, and in particular young companies such as start-ups, where one or more founders maintain disproportionate power and influence following the effective initial establishment of the organization, leading to a wide range of problems. The syndrome occurs in both non-profit and for-profit organizations or companies."[18]

On this same Wikipedia page, symptoms of Founder's Syndrome are described as:

- "The organization is strongly identified with the founder; a result sometimes believed to be related to the founder's ego."

- "Obsessive leadership style compared to a more standard behavior."

- "Autocratic decision-making (autocratic management style): Founders tend to make all decisions in early start-up companies, big and small, without a formal process or feedback from others. Decisions are made in crisis mode, with little forward planning. Staff meetings are held generally to rally the troops, get status reports, and assign tasks. There is little meaningful strategic development, or shared executive agreement on objectives with limited or a complete lack of professional development. Typically,

---

[18] https://en.wikipedia.org/wiki/Founder's_syndrome

there is little organizational infrastructure in place, and what is there is not used correctly. Furthermore, the founder has difficulty making decisions that benefit the organization because of their affiliation."

- "Higher levels of micromanagement by checking on employees['] or colleagues['] subject matter work instead of maintaining and evolving the overall company's picture."

- "Entrepreneurs show higher levels of bias (e.g. over-confidence) than do managers in established organizations."

- "There is no succession plan."

- "A failing so-called *leadership transition* within [the] first couple of years leading to consequences such as trust, morale, [or] unforeseen future for the business."

- "The founder has difficulty with adapting to changes as the organization matures."

- "The culture of the leadership team and company plays an important role for success or failure."

- "Often the founder's idea is central to the initial business and clients of the company, so that if markets change, the need for the initial idea might vanish."

- "Key staff and board members are typically selected by the founder and are often friends and colleagues of the founder. Their role is to support the founder, rather than to lead the mission. Staff may be chosen due to their personal loyalty to the founder rather than skills, organizational fit, or experience. Board members may be under-qualified, under-informed or intimidated and will typically be unable to answer basic questions without checking first."

- "Professionally trained and talented recruits, often recruited to resolve difficulties in the organization, find that they are not able to contribute in an effective and professional way."
- "The founder begins to believe their own press/PR and other marketing related issues."
- "The founder, who is usually the CEO or managing director, suffers *HiPPO* (Highest-paid-person's opinion), which means that often their ideas, decisions, etc. keep winning over the actual better ideas, decisions, etc."
- "The founder becomes increasingly paranoid as delegation is required, or business management needs are greater than their training or experience."
- "Falling into two traps:
    - "Actions without a goal *or*
    - "Wrong actions based on defined goal."

Even further, the description goes on to state, "founder responds to increasingly challenging issues by accentuating the above, leading to further difficulties. Anyone who challenges this cycle will be treated as a disruptive influence and will be ignored, ridiculed or removed. The working environment will be increasingly difficult with decreasing trust. The organization becomes increasingly reactive, rather than proactive. Alternatively, the founder or the board may recognize the issue and take effective action."[19]

Now that you know a bit about first-time founder CEOs if you haven't yet experienced it firsthand, let me tell you a story.

---

[19] https://en.wikipedia.org/wiki/Founder's_syndrome

Before COVID-19 came on the scene hard, I was working with a tech company that was trying to navigate through an interesting problem and how to disrupt it, as so many tech companies are.

The start-up had been around for a few years, had a small team of fewer than fifty, and they were looking to grow.

We've worked with many growth companies before, helping them to figure out how to scale without losing themselves and their core values, and honestly, working with what makes their company unique.

So we were brought in to work with this company, and after talking to several people who worked there, we felt the foundation was good.

Now, for most start-ups, especially those with first-time founders, I absolutely have to note that having a solid foundation built is a major rarity. Most of the time, there isn't even a semblance of one to start on, yet they think there is, and they start building anyway, only to see it topple over "unexpectedly" after a year or two because they didn't take the time to properly support the foundation of the business and the culture.

But this start-up really *did* have a good foundation. Their employees really enjoyed working there. They loved their jobs. They loved the people they worked with. They trusted and believed in leadership. They didn't all look the same (which was also a great foundational item that very rarely happens in early start-up days), and they encouraged new thoughts and ideas. In short, it was a small but mighty team, supporting each other, making a difference, and loving what they did nine days out of ten.

But they needed to grow in order to be successful on a balance sheet and in order to be able to help make a bigger impact on their mission.

We were brought in to help them on the talent side to set up technology and processes to scale as well as diving into the actual recruiting. We helped build out the total team from fifty to nearly 400 in a two-year span.

We had hit our stride early with this company, and it was easy to see that what we were doing was impactful. We saw that what we were building was different, that it was truly making a difference in the world, that people loved working together in the culture that was built early and thoughtfully, and that the growth had been carefully monitored.

But then, about a year and a half in, things started to change.

The first-time founder and CEO was absent for a lot of the time because he had to go and raise additional funding. He brought in an executive from one of the large tech companies to run things while he was gone.

But this was where the mistake happened.

This company, built from scrappiness, resourcefulness, kindness, and appreciation for people from all backgrounds, thoughts, and perspectives as well as race, religion, ethnicity, gender orientation, gender expression, etc., was as close to a perfect working environment as I think we can achieve as humans who all have flaws.

There is no perfect human work environment because culture is made up by people, and there is no perfect person.

But this place was close—super close—and everyone knew it. They knew what we had was good, really good. Tension-off-of-your-shoulders good.

We-had-hard-problems-but-we-could-figure-them-out-together good.

I-trust-you-and-have-your-back-like-you've-got-mine good.

I-want-to-hear-what-you-have-to-say-that's-dissenting good.

I'm telling you—it was nearly 24k gold. So nearly.

But the CEO didn't take enough time to actually realize what was needed. He needed to stay. He was a motivator. He was inspirational. He knew the people in the company, and the people trusted and cared for him.

But instead, he left, and he left a "new babysitter" in charge.

The "new babysitter" didn't know us. We didn't know her. She knew nearly nothing about the company and its people and what we had built together.

Frankly, she seemed not to care at all about what was already in place or the people who had been there.

It was very clear from the first time our team met her that she wanted to make this place the next FAANG.

Now, as an executive myself, I know that Management 101 tells you to get to know your new company, the people, what's working, what's not, etc., but she didn't take the time to do this.

In fewer than six months, the culture tumbled. I left early in our consulting agreement with them. (They'd asked me to actually extend it, and I declined.)

The amazing people who helped build the organization and made it great mostly all left.

The time I had worked to help build up this amazing organization, helping to elevate it but keeping the same core values and vision alive, had crumbled with one toxic employee.

One bad hire can cause an entire company to fall, especially if that hire is in the executive ranks. Every move of a toxic executive is amplified across the organization.

And there was no mistaking that she thought none of us knew anything, and that she knew absolutely everything. She was disrespectful, insensitive, and knew nothing of the context she should have used to make her decisions.

One example in particular sticks out in my mind. In this culture I had helped shape and build to its magnificence, we all felt we could bring our whole selves to work. People would say that often—people in URGs would say it. It was felt that it was okay to be yourself and to let others know who you were, truly.

But during one meeting with this new executive, one of my colleagues wore a shirt that she loved featuring one of her favorite singers. This new executive made a weird comment about the shirt—I can't remember the exact wording she used but it was something very flippant like, "To each their own." This executive had also commented on how tough it was for her, a white woman in America, as she took Zoom calls with her Peloton bike in the background.

How horrible are we, white women? You really want to talk about how "bad you have it" in a virtual room full of people in URGs and with a $2,000 exercise bike in the background?

Again, wow!

Today, as I write this, I hold fast to my belief that this person destroyed the culture, but I also blame the first-time founder and CEO because he wanted to grow too fast. And that greed, that desire to be the next unicorn, killed the culture of the company. It became everything wrong with Corporate America, almost overnight. Their mission today is full of empty words and promises.

The first-time founder CEO intimately knew the organization, the mission, and had helped build the near-perfect foundation with an impactful mission at the early stages, but like a lot of early-stage start-ups, he ignored all of that to bring in the shiny thing from a large tech company because he thought it looked better on the masthead for possible investors.

He did what a lot of first-time founder CEOs do—he forgot why he was doing this.

Or maybe he didn't forget, and maybe he manipulated people the whole way through, but knowing him, I honestly don't think that was the case.

A lot of first-time founder CEOs aren't realistic or don't think early enough about the exit strategy. And I get it, they spend so much time building and making their business work that they can't think far enough ahead to focus on what the exit strategy should be. But that's a mistake, and one I've seen time and time again.

If you are looking to build a company up to run it forever and have it remain a private company, you invest more in people and foundations than if you want to build it quickly to sell it fast. The exit strategy has an immense impact on the way a business is built.

But first-time founder CEOs should be way more open with their executive teams and their employees on what that is. Too many of them hold those conversations only behind closed doors, and that's a mistake. That's why layoffs happen, that's why offices close, that's why people get pissed—and rightly so.

By being upfront and honest with an exit strategy from the start, a first-time founder CEO is also way more honest when it comes to allowing employees to properly evaluate the equity and options they have. The CEOs who try to "sell" one type of culture, only to rip it away because an appealing new exit strategy came along, are doing a disservice to their employees because those employees may have been counting on equity and options when realistically there was no value there to be had because that wasn't the ultimate exit strategy for the CEO.

It happens. It happens all the time.

And until you experience being in an organization like this, you have no idea what you are entering.

Another common mistake that first-time founder CEOs face is being too in the weeds for too long. They micromanage constantly and for everything. No one in the organization is allowed to make a decision, even a tiny one, without the CEO checking it off first.

That's bad all the way around.

It not only undermines all of the expertise that you bring in the door—not to mention all of the salaries you are paying those individuals—but it also puts too much on the CEO's plate, and what I've seen is that they get mean, they get defensive, they get combative, and then they burn out.

By micromanaging, these first-time founder CEOs also never allow anyone to truly help intertwine the business units internally. There is never trust that is built or given between executive team members or even between departments. Everyone is always trying to vie for the CEO's time because they know that the ultimate decision lands at the CEO's feet.

And even worse is when a first-time founder CEO tries to micromanage everything, has no prior experience in most of the business workings, and then won't listen to any expertise along the way or absorb it in any fashion.

That's a very dangerous way to lead a business.

If that's what you want to do as a first-time founder CEO, you might as well save yourself and the business a lot of time and money, and just hire zero other executives or business leaders in the organization. Because when you do hire experts in their fields, they will get so fed up so quickly, that it will be a revolving door of leaders, and then the teams under those leaders will have a continual cycle of trying to understand a new leader, filling that new leader in, starting to gain comfort and trust, and then having the rug pulled out from under them yet again. So then team members leave because they are fed up.

The biggest way to tank a business from the inside out is to micromanage and listen to no one.

And honestly, I myself have been in the position of trying to get a first-time founder CEO to see how taking items off of their plate isn't the end of the world—and trusting the executives who were hired to do their jobs—all to have the CEO try to push me out the door as quickly as possible. And the same proves true for anyone like me who was trying to drive real change in the organization.

To any investor, this should be a major red flag. Especially if an organization goes through more than one C-suite executive in a year; if they go through four C-suite executives in *one* department in the same year, you know the CEO has Founderitis.

Many first-time founder CEOs also try to be everything to everyone, and that never works either.

Think about it—when does that actually work? It doesn't. It never works.

And by the way, not all first-time founder CEOs are bad. Some of them are better than the others, but it is very rare.

The best first-time founder CEOs I've worked with have been self-aware enough to know what they are good at, bringing experts in to do what they are not good at, and then listening to their guidance—all without having to be a decision maker on anything that is related to certain departments or anything company-wide that that leader may know more about. These are the stellar ones, the ones that make businesses better. They are also the CEOs people follow from business to business after that because they feel respected and valued.

For most first-time founder CEOs, they try to build something that hasn't existed before or a new way of doing things, but they also try to create a better work environment than they have experienced. But therein lie the details that matter—they try to create work environments when they have never actually built a work environment before. The smart ones leave it up to the experts who have experience in the building of great work environments.

In the Revolution of Work, we really can't keep funneling the most money toward white male founders and expecting things to be different. Investors keep pumping money into white men, many of whom have absolutely no experience managing people and teams, and we wonder why disengagement scores keep rising and people hate work so much.

So, if you're reading this book as a first-time founder CEO and you do exhibit any of the Founderitis elements mentioned above, I hope you can recognize it and be big enough to ask for help. And then listen to the help provided and act on it. Your team, your leaders, and your employees will thank you. And you just might save your business from disaster.

And investors, please, for all of the love, you absolutely *should* be giving chances and money to more and more people who aren't white men. In fact, it just may make you more money in doing so, since a lot of founders who aren't white men actually have experience managing people and running businesses; you may not have heard about them because they just haven't had the same advantages as the white men.

Chapter 9

COMPENSATION— THE STATUS QUO ONLY HELPS WHITE PEOPLE

No matter how you spin it, the world revolves around money. And the people with the most money wield the most power, and in the US, the wealthiest people are white men who tend to hold up the patriarchy because it benefits them. By continuing to act like compensation isn't at the heart of it all with organizations, those already privileged and in power remain so and keep everyone else down.

In the Revolution of Work, compensation helps to change this. But in order for the revolution to happen, the way that candidates, employees, and business owners and leaders look at money must change.

Let me tell you a story about a former colleague of mine.

This colleague absolutely outworked every other man in her department. She also had the knowledge and expertise to do the jobs of those in the positions above her.

But when it came time for a promotion and salary increase, she was consistently met with hedging, false promises, and the common phrases those in URGs often hear: "We just can't do that right now."

This colleague was a top performer, always in the top 5 percent of the company in every performance review. She was well regarded among colleagues, both at executive levels and throughout the organization.

But when it came to increasing workloads across her department, she was always asked to take on more. Her salary increases never equaled that of her white hetero cis male colleagues.

In fact, she was the only one in her department consistently putting in sixty to eighty hours per week.

After discussing with other colleagues in the organization, she realized that in her years at this organization, others had gotten significant salary increases when they asked for them, sometimes $10,000 to $50,000 at one time.

Yet, those talking to her about compensation kept saying that the organization "didn't have it."

Middle finger to the sky.

One day, one of our other colleagues, who had boasted at a happy hour about getting a $25k increase and a title bump "for no extra work," came over to her to ask for a favor. He needed help fixing a mistake that he had made in his role. The colleague helped him, and afterward, he said, "You know, you're really not paid enough."

This story isn't rare. It's not unique.

My colleague had shown that she could do the job of her boss and her boss's boss. Yet, every time she advocated for herself, she never got what she asked for. She felt taken advantage of by the organization, and she didn't feel entirely seen and valued.

This situation is the reason why so many people in URGs quit their jobs.

And by the way, the organization clearly *could* give increases in large quantities because they had, and she knew they had! But those who got it? White men.

In this example alone, the $25,000 increase that our other colleague boasted he received compounds—negatively for the woman not receiving it and positively for the man who did receive it. In fact, the woman had higher level roles previously in her career than the man had in his role, yet the organization was so quick to give him a $25,000 increase.

And you want to know the real kick-in-the-pants? He didn't even ask for that much.

He asked for a $10,000 increase.

So one woman is advocating for herself, doing more than her full job, able to do the job two levels above her, and everyone rates her highly, yet she doesn't receive what she advocates for? And the white man who came to her to fix a mistake, asked for $10,000 and they gave him $25,000?

Come on! And we wonder why compensation is always a sensitive issue for people? It's because most organizations do things like this. It's the norm, not the exception.

Even if we back up a bit and talk about new hires coming into a company, women and men even apply to roles differently.

Women tend to apply to roles that they meet 90-100 percent of requirements for (and the data shows that the same goes for other marginalized community members, too), but men tend to apply to roles that they meet 40-60 percent of the requirements for.

Then, once people go through interviewing processes, and offers are made, women and people in URGs tend to negotiate less for their starting salaries.

The story I'm about to tell is quite minimal comparably. Yet it showcases just a glimpse of what happens every day in Corporate America.

I was talking to a recruiter during an interview process many years ago.

The recruiter told me about the salary for the role during our first call—which was great and should be done in all initial phone calls during an interview process.

But a surprise came when this company sent me an offer letter. And it wasn't a good surprise.

I was out of town when I received the offer letter and didn't have great access to Wi-Fi, so I was looking at the offer on my phone.

The offer letter had a salary for the role at $5,000 less than I was quoted. So I called the recruiter and told her that I believed the salary was incorrect on the offer letter.

Her response? No, the offer letter was correct. And the misquoting of the initial salary was her mistake. She then brushed me off and said, "It's only a $5,000 difference. It's not that big of a deal."

The salary for this role was under $50,000, so actually, at that point in my life, $5,000 *was* a big deal.

I told her that I was taken aback by the miscommunication, and that the change in salary was in fact a big deal to me but I was very much interested in the role and the company and the impact I could make. So, I asked her if she could go back to the team and see if she could make good on the initial offer.

She then proceeded to plead with me, saying that she "didn't want to get in trouble" and that she'd "look bad" in front of her boss.

And yes, this woman is a white woman.

I told her that I'd happily sign for an offer of $50,000, which was $5,000 more than the original offer she had verbally quoted to me from the beginning, albeit the one that I later realized was the incorrect salary number.

She then started to get defensive. She said, "Well if you don't want the job, you need to tell me now."

The candidate experience completely changed, by my asking for $5,000 more than what was originally quoted. I then added, "Well if $5,000 wasn't a big deal five minutes ago when you gave that number to me, then $5,000 shouldn't be a big deal now when I'm asking to increase the starting salary."

Silence.

I let the silence linger because before this, I was a journalist, and I knew how to let silence linger so people fill the void with more information than they ever intended to give you from the outset.

For one whole minute and twenty seconds, there was silence. Then, she said she would check back with the team and get back to me.

Not five minutes later, she sent me a text that said the lower salary—$40,000—was the salary that was being offered.

Although I know now that that was an early red flag of the company's culture, I didn't know that then, and I wanted the job, so I took it.

Looking back on it, I am enraged by the behavior of this woman, who is a high-level People leader now.

Later interactions with her would prove the same as they did that day, that she was in the job for one person and one person only: herself.

I wish I had known then to walk away.

But women tend to do that.

We tend to take what we are given, even when we ask for more.

We smile and say, "Thank you," because that's how society has told us we should be. At least that's how my generation was taught.

We were taught to be polite and nice because if not, we were too confident and too direct.

Back to my white privilege: I'm wholeheartedly glad that my parents, my mom especially, taught me to stand up for what I believe in, to be loud about it, to never take no for an answer, and to be direct. And if that gets you labeled a bitch for truth telling, then so be it.

Side note: When I was growing up, when my mother would get called a bitch, she'd stop, look right at the person, take a breath of silence, and then say, "I'm not a bitch, I'm *the* bitch. Get it right."

Yet somehow in my youth, as with most of us, I didn't have as much gumption as I would have liked.

Now in my middle age, I know what I'm worth, I know what I want to stand for, and I don't compromise on any of it. My speaking up and speaking out doesn't necessarily help me, but it helps others who don't look like me.

Compensation is one of those areas that negatively compounds the more you go through life if you're a woman or in a URG. It's like investing in a company with compound interest, but in reverse for those who are not white cis men.

Think about it:

If I started out with my first full-time job being paid $24,000 a year, while the men counterparts were likely paid nearly $29,000, then in my next role, I'm paid $40,000, while the men counterparts are paid $48,000, and when I work my way up to being paid $68,000, the men counterparts were likely paid almost $82,000. For me, that time span was over six years. In those six years, I went from $24,000/yr. to $68,000/yr., making a rough total of $220,000. Meanwhile, over those six years, it is likely that the men counterparts made a total of a little more than $265,000. That means that spread across six years, men likely made $7,500 more than me per year. (And this is a conservative example. Many times, the compounding effect of compensation is far worse than this.)

It's worse for women who aren't white—and even for men who aren't white. Compound that advantage over a thirty-year career, and in this example, white men would have "earned" more than $225,000 more than me if I had stayed at those salary levels. And on what basis?

Add to that the cost-of-living adjustments (COLA) that some companies give their employees, and that 3 percent to 6 percent of salaries compound, too. And 6 percent of $82,000 is more than 6 percent of $68,000.

Consider this, Black women will make $1,000,000 less than white men over their lifetimes.[20]

Come on, y'all!

Even the most pragmatic among you have to realize this is ridiculous.

With this foundational layer of compensation being so drastically fucked up, you can see how the money deck keeps stacking higher and higher for the privileged and the deck keeps getting stacked against those without privilege or without as much privilege as others.

Compensation is just the first layer.

White men also get looked at for the most promotions, then white women, and so on—and those who aren't white have to work extra hard and longer to even get the opportunity to be seen at all for their expertise or work, let alone be promoted into higher roles.

And for those who aren't white, you can work your ass off, do all the right things, have all the right experience, and still not get the next title or role or promotion because of the biased culture we live in.

Time and time again in my career, I've seen those in URGs who have done the job, sometimes for months or years, but have

---

[20] According to this 2021 article on CNBC: https://www.cnbc.com/2021/08/03/black-women-make-1-million-less-than-white-men-during-their-careers.html

never been given the title. So they do all the work without earning the pay they should have.

Years ago, we were working with a client who was looking to grow exponentially. They were looking at massive growth and wanted to be the next unicorn or rocket ship in tech (which by the way, if you ever hear that, run the other way—you'll thank me!).

They were looking to hire someone for a niche role that doesn't really exist in many companies today, yet I knew someone who would have been absolutely perfect for this role like it was written specifically for her.

This woman was so supremely qualified and would have elevated both the role and the company. In fact, she would have absolutely nailed it.

Yet when the head of talent looked at her résumé, she said that this woman "didn't look like she had enough experience."

I nearly spit out my drink when she said that.

"Who?"

I had to make sure she and I were talking about the same person.

When she told me she just didn't think this person had the skills needed in the role, I then explained all of the roles she had had at levels higher than this role—and then some that she performed but was never given the title for.

I then asked the head of talent if she spoke to my referral, and she said, "No, I was just going off of her résumé."

And there you have it, folks. Gatekeeping at its finest. White privilege much? This head of talent didn't even pick up the phone to ask questions of this person to gain more knowledge.

She just wrote her off without a second thought based on a piece of paper. And we wonder why recruiters and interview processes get such a bad reputation for bias? This is why. Bad recruiters and horrible leaders like this head of talent.

Meanwhile, the hiring manager for the role and I had a conversation, and she said she really wanted to speak to my referral because she sounded perfect for the role.

What did the head of talent do? She purposefully extended the interview process and made this person jump through hoops in hopes that my referral would drop out on their own.

Well, guess what happened? The woman I referred pulled out of the process. She saw right through all of the crap that the head of talent was spewing about a culture in support of DEI because she herself wasn't even showcasing needed support of DEI.

This happens too frequently.

Horrible recruiters and talent acquisition professionals gatekeep, and they absolutely should be doing the opposite. In my experience, those talent professionals who gatekeep are truly trying to cover up insecurity or a resistance to change.

Talent professionals who are constantly learning new and better ways to recruit all humans (especially those from marginalized groups) and trying new and amazing technologies are those who are at the forefront of their industry. One of the great differentiators of great talent professionals is the ability to understand where the candidate is coming from while understanding the candidate's experience and giving them fair market value from a salary perspective up front.

Time and time again in my early career—I'm dating myself, but I started in recruiting actively in 2010 but had done recruiting prior to that without understanding what it was all the way back in 2008—I found recruiters talking about "getting that candidate for a steal."

It always felt icky to me.

Number one, who is talking about "getting candidates" like they are baseball cards? People are not something to collect, and you shouldn't be trying to get them for a steal. If you are, get out of any of the professions that have anything to do with people immediately because you are a horrible human being.

Full stop.

Getting people for a steal is a control mechanism rooted in colonialism as a way for white people to continue to keep other races down.

Getting people for a steal isn't doing DEIJ work—in fact, it is the exact opposite.

Getting people for a steal is unkind and frankly inhumane.

Getting people for a steal is something that can tell me far more about the person recruiting and reveal so much about an organization in a very short time frame—and none of what that is revealing is even remotely good.

People have value. Their skill sets have worth. You should absolutely, unequivocally never be trying to "get people for a steal."

Why would you want to?

Do you really want one of the first impressions of your organization to be one of cheapskates? Or to be one of not understanding the value that people are to your organization?

I can't tell you how many "People-first" organizations pay people horribly and try to "get people for a steal." I've even seen recruiters jumping around and laughing about how they were able to get someone for $10,000 under starting salary. Why is this a celebration? Why is this a victory? Does $10,000 really mean that much to your business, and if so, should you be hiring at all because that makes me question your company's financial stability? Shouldn't a person feel ashamed by that behavior and the act of

---

demoting a person to a lower salary? Do people really act this way? Yes, they do. And unfortunately, there are far too many talent professionals out there who act this way. Or they try to rationalize their compensation by saying that the company doesn't have a ton of money or "we're still in early stages."

If a company has money to operate, it has money to pay people well. If a company has money to pay executives, you better damn sure believe that it has money to pay people well. If a company is making millions or billions in revenue, it absolutely has money to pay people well. In fact, those talent professionals and executives who like to try to get people in at lower salary levels than they ask are often the ones making $100K+ and trying to keep more of the profits for themselves.

Again, it's a control mechanism.

Compensation can either add to your DEIJ efforts, or it can deteriorate them quickly. By paying people well, you put your literal money where your mouth is and your DEIJ efforts will be boosted. If you pay people less than what they are asking, you are cutting your DEIJ efforts short and really devastating any trust that candidates have toward you before they even step foot in the door.

And while we are on the topics of interviewing and candidate experience, please stop wasting candidates' time.

Compensation is paying someone for their time or their skill set.

If you are going to require more than four interviews—yep I said four—total for any interview process that is any role other than a C-suite role, then you need to do one of two things:

1) Cut your process way down. Decide who absolutely needs to be in the interview and remove everyone else. Set up structured hiring for the interview, and make sure that all of your interviewers and hiring managers understand expectations for them in the process and make sure they have all had interviewer training prior to any interviews.

2) Pay people for their time. Ask them what their hourly rate is and pay them for additional interviews.

For C-suite hires, you should also absolutely be cutting down your processes. There is no reason that C-suite hires should take months—and most of them take three to eighteen months to complete. C-suite interview processes should include no more than five hours' worth of interviews. A good rule of thumb to remember here is that C-suite interview processes should be a max of twice the amount of time that someone who isn't interviewing for C-suite should experience—so if you have a max of two and a half hours for a non-C-suite role, then your C-suite role interview process should be a max of five hours.

> If you pay people less than what they are asking, you are cutting your DEIJ efforts short and really devastating any trust that candidates have toward you before they even step foot in the door.

In that same realm, most C-suite executive interviews also typically include some sort of ninety-day plan or SWOT (strengths, weaknesses, opportunities, and threats) analysis. This is work. This is knowledge and expertise that a person is providing for an organization. You are asking a candidate to do strategy work—and that should be paid. If you are asking for a ninety-day plan, great executives are going to need more time with executives to ask them questions in order to gain enough insight to give you a real ninety-day plan—which means taking more time away from your current executives' work and more time in the process for everyone involved.

I've even heard many horror stories of these ninety-day plans making their way into the company's strategic roadmap—and when you aren't paying for this work—you are *stealing* the candidate's ideas.

In fact, stop asking people for free work, period.

There are tons of companies out there that ask UX (user experience) and product designers to design something for the interview process or ask engineers to code something for the interview process.

Data has shown that these assessments really do not determine how well these candidates are actually going to perform or how they actually are at their jobs.

So why do we keep doing it?

It's the same reason companies continue to ask for more and more interviews—and take more and more time in the process. The ones that are doing the interviewing: 1) are horrible at interviewing; 2) were never properly trained to interview well; 3) lack the confidence to make decisions because they feel insecure about their interviewing abilities; or 4) fear failure so much that they feel paralyzed about making the wrong decision to hire someone.

Here's the little secret that very few people in the talent profession will tell you—nine times out of ten, we get it right, but there is always that one out of every ten that we get wrong. The reason? We are trying to gauge a fully-formed human being on their vast experience levels in a small time frame—and we are going on what they tell us as truth. We do the best we can in gauging these elements—and recruiters are better at this than most people because we have honed this craft—but we are not machines. We will not get it right 100 percent of the time because we are humans judging humans. On both sides of the equation, there are human beings with flaws and imperfections.

And guess what? That's okay.

Instead of having this enormous fear of making the wrong decision when it comes to hiring, just decide and understand that one out of every ten may be the wrong one. But with the right experts in place in your Talent and People teams, you will know how to address that quickly, and how to find the right person for the job. By expecting that instead of being surprised by it, the weight of the decision becomes lighter.

And since we are on the topic of asking candidates to do free work, let's also talk about another common mistake that most companies and most company leaders make—not paying the employees in their organizations for time spent working on ERGs (employee resource groups).

If you are a company that wants to truly go down the path of making the organization one that is more focused on providing a safe and enjoyable work environment for all humans, then you may be thinking about ERGs, if you don't already have them.

But here is the thing with ERGs—DO NOT JUST CHECK A BOX!

Checking a box with ERGs looks like this:

- Starting an ERG.

- Asking marginalized groups within your organization to work on these ERGs.

- Not compensating them fairly, or at all, for their time and lived experiences.

- Not providing ERGs substantive budgets, or any, to do real work.

- Not wanting to change anything in the organization.

- Not listening to anything the ERGs present or ask for.

If you are not ready to dedicate at least an hourly rate per hour worked for every member of the ERG above and beyond their salaries—or by providing them a significant bonus above and beyond that amount—and you don't have a minimum of $10,000 per year for each ERG, then you are likely doing more harm than good by trying to provide this to your organization.

Also—let's be real—if you want to start ERGs or even have ERGs in your org, and you don't compensate people and the ERG above at least as stated, then you are supremely kidding yourself that you are realistic about improving your work environment for all humans but specifically traditionally marginalized groups.

In fact, by not providing compensation—or *enough* compensation—to the individual and the group itself, you are actually making things worse because you are asking the people who have been marginalized to do more work for no extra money. You could have just saved them time and not had them do extra work for no extra money—or not enough extra money.

I remember a company we worked with a few years back that so desperately wanted to have ERGs in their organization.

Yet, the white people didn't roll up their sleeves to try to understand what was needed. They instead "voluntold" those in marginalized groups that they had to establish ERGs.

Let's be real. Isn't that just colonialism in a different sense? Asking people from already marginalized groups to do the work for those who are actually the ones who *need* to do the work? Isn't this exactly what happened when John Smith came over from England and then "worked with" American Indians to farm? Do you think they elected to do that? Or do you think they were scared for their lives, so they decided to do what the colonizer told them to do in order to stay alive?

Don't do what that company did.

If you are going to put these items in place, then pay appropriately—and then sit down, shut up, and listen…then act and help clear pathways for the voices you want to elevate. Make sure you actually change the dynamics of your environment if you are going to ask people to add their own time into an ERG. Don't let them down by dropping the baton at the end of the race.

Still, unpaid and free work asked for by companies doesn't end here. Many companies ask salaried employees to take on more and more work, especially after layoffs because we all know that the work doesn't lighten when a layoff happens. The work post-layoff typically just moves to another person's already full plate.

As a company or company leader, please get it out of your head that you *own* any semblance of an employee's time—and that if you pay them a salary for forty hours, you can work them for eighty hours a week. For those of you who do this, I'm not sure how you sleep at night. If you have employees who are consistently working sixty-to-eighty hours a week, you should be paying them one and a half to two times their salary! And if you aren't, you are "getting them for a steal." In essence, you are stealing their time.

I'm not sure how anyone feels good and right about that, but many companies think it's fine and believe it's how you do business. It's not. Stop it. It's called control and power, and you're not using your authority for good in that moment.

In fact, if you try to get candidates "for cheap," ask interviewers to spend six hours in interviews, ask candidates to submit free work, ask people to start and continue ERGs without proper compensation or any compensation at all, and ask salaried employees to consistently (as in more than like three weeks a year) work for sixty to eighty hours a week, you better not in any circumstance ever say that you treat people well or that you are a people-first company or that you care for your employees or that you support DEIJ—because all of those are lies.

You can do better. If you do any of the items that I just stated to your employees or candidates, you should *want* to do better.

Think about it—you are fine with asking a candidate to take more time in an interview process. You're fine with asking people to work double what is considered full time per week. Yet you scoff when someone asks you to compensate them fairly? How does that make any sense?

If you go to the grocery store, and you take four pounds of strawberries instead of two—do you have to pay more for them? Absolutely.

If you buy artisan bread instead of a factory-produced loaf, do you pay more for it? Sure.

So if you are okay with these purchases at your local grocery store, how in the world are you not okay with treating people as human beings? You treat strawberries and bread better than people.

Make it make sense.

And if you are in People or Human Resources, compensation falls on you most of the time. I get it. I've been there.

For the love of all that is good—please, please, pretty please, bring in a compensation consultant if you don't know what you are doing. If you have done it once and have only seen one compensation cycle, please bring in a consultant. There are myriad ways to do compensation well, and to be fair, out of the thousands of People professionals I have met over my career, I only know a handful who truly understand and know how to do compensation right.

Compensation is not something to do with a half-assed approach. It is important. It is money that goes to people to pay for the food on their tables, for their kids' summer camps, for their family's medical needs, etc. Compensation is highly important. Please make sure you are giving it the importance it warrants by getting an expert to help you.

Over the years, I've seen compensation done poorly at most organizations. There are very few and far between that actually look at compensation correctly and provide proper value for people in their organization—and even fewer that look at compensation as an equitable device across the organization.

Done well, compensation can truly enliven your DEIJ strategies. It is the basis of most DEIJ work, yet most leaders push it off as an afterthought.

Years ago, I worked at an organization that was known for being at the cutting edge of People and Culture trends.

At that time, I was part of the team looking at compensation and how to do it better than everyone else. We looked across the industry and other industries and wanted to do it the best anyone had ever done it. What we didn't know at the time was that we were far ahead of the curve. We were doing roles-based compensation.

Now, for those of you not in HR and not familiar, roles-based compensation is based on the level and role within the organization, and then looking at market data for that role, instead of trying to gauge the subjective nature of what that role is worth in your own organization.

Performance also wasn't tied to compensation levels and roles from a salary perspective. Performance was assessed every quarter, plus weekly by managers, and when a person met the level to get promoted in the org, they were able to gain that promotion and the salary change every quarter.

And at the end of the year, if the company did well, there was profit-sharing across the organization.

By looking at roles-based compensation, you aren't giving more money to the white guy who knows the founder. You are giving the same compensation to those who have the same role and are at the same level. Less bias goes into compensation this way. And, if you aren't aware, most other forms of compensation strategy have an immense amount of subjective bias attached. Roles-based compensation is one of the best ways to drive equality across organizations.

But I realize getting most organizations to a level of equality is difficult.

It does take a lot of time and effort to put a process in place and to maintain it, and it takes a lot of money to keep up with it.

But if you do it well and keep up with it, I've seen that it can be a competitive advantage and you actually end up saving money because you have less of a revolving door of people in and out of your organization. And you also have more people who stay because they feel respected and fairly compensated—and they see their path up and forward.

Now, for those of you who are really progressive, and really inclined to truly do compensation differently, I'd like to take it one step further.

Leaders who truly want to lead the pack in compensation and DEIJ should be looking at not only equal compensation but equitable compensation.

If you haven't yet seen the data of how much less people in URGs make than white men, you must be living under a rock.

There are years and years of compounded inequities in compensation for those who aren't white men. And for the white men, they've had hundreds of years of compounded advantage over everyone else.

So truly progressive organizations, I believe, will be looking at driving equity compensation, meaning that those who are not white cis men should be given higher compensation than their white cis men counterparts to help balance the scales. And I know how much this will take—it will be an immense amount of balancing and years upon years that are needed to compound to make a difference here—but if we don't start and look at this from this angle, pay gaps will only widen. This is one of the ways we can actually work to close it.

Before the white men come for me, think about all of the tremendous privilege you have had in your life. Compensation is only one of those factors. Is it really that bad to allow others to feel as well compensated as you?

Compensation is truly that important because compensation affects mental well-being, health outcomes, childcare, marital status, and every aspect of life. It's not just about your salary; the dollars in the bank are what you either build a life upon or scrape by with. For too many years, the deck has been stacked against the individual versus the company, and even more so for those from marginalized groups.

As companies, as leaders, as people *looking* for new companies and leaders—we should all be looking at ways to get real and get right with compensation so that the scales balance out.

There is no need for white cis men and companies to have trick cards up their sleeves anymore.

We can all win at the game if we are all playing by the same rules. The patriarchy has been playing by its own rules for far too long. It's time to literally spread the wealth.

Chapter 10

FEEDBACK—
WE'RE ALL PRETTY
HORRIBLE AT IT

"You are too good at your job."

"We would be lost without you."

"You are too direct."

"You make your other colleagues feel uncomfortable with the knowledge and expertise you bring to the table."

"You are years ahead of your age."

"You are too good looking to be that smart."

"You should keep your head down more and blend into the background."

"You always run circles around us, and we're going to need you to stop doing that so the rest of the leaders can catch up."

"You are intimidating."

"You are condescending."

"You're confident."

These are all pieces of feedback that I've heard over my career.

As a woman who has been at many executive tables where I am the only one, after the first few times, it was almost expected for me to hear things like this.

I became conditioned to expect to hear it.

I'm guessing that most women or people in URGs in my position, by being the only one that looks like you at the table, have also experienced this. I guess this because I've talked to hundreds of people who have told me just that.

But the feedback is never helpful. It's never something that is actionable or even reasonable.

Most people are providing feedback wrong. In fact, most people do it fucking horribly. Hell, if I had listened to even an ounce of this ridiculous feedback, I wouldn't be where I am today.

I'm a fairly confident person. I understand who I am, I try to remain self-aware, and I continue to learn to get better at things I'm not so good at. And I check in with people, including my personal board of directors, often. They're my support group, and they aren't afraid to tell me ugly truths. I surround myself with people who are not yes-men, yes-women, and yes-nonbinary folx because I want to hear my flaws and what I can do better, but from people who know me and understand me in a fuller and broader sense.

Often the people who see you clearly are those in your circle, and they at times can see you better than you can even see yourself.

But most people aren't confident and secure, and they don't take the time often enough to look at themselves to see how they can get better, if at all. So, when they hear comments like these above, it can tear them down to their core and cause them to rethink their entire jobs, career, and lives.

We all need feedback to get better, but here's the thing—when people in URGs hear feedback, it is almost always a direct projection or symptom of insecurity of the feedback giver than it is about the person receiving the feedback.

When people give feedback, most try too hard to be nice instead of being kind, especially in the US. Kindness is about being clear and providing communication in a way that the receiver can understand while also caring deeply about the person. Being nice is a default that most of us resort to when we are nervous or uncomfortable, but being nice tends to stop the true message from clearly coming out. Often niceness causes people to hold back when giving feedback that would actually be helpful and actionable to the person receiving it.

I remember one of my first jobs, and my boss at the time wanted to chat about my performance. We didn't typically do annual reviews but tried to do more frequent reviews of performance across the company. I can't quite remember exactly what was provided to each person ahead of time, but I can remember preparing my thoughts about my work and writing them down. I had prepared for weeks to have this discussion. I knew I had thirty minutes to chat with him about what I wanted in my career and questions I wanted to ask him regarding how he thought it was best for me to achieve these items. I also brought examples of the work I had done that was outside of the scope of my job and above and beyond what was asked of me.

As the discussion started, my boss told me that he had no feedback for me, that I was doing amazing work. While some people would think, "Right, brilliant! Okay, thanks!" I felt disappointed. I was waiting to be given more direction and guidance and help to understand what I missed the mark on, even if just a little, so that I had areas to improve upon in my role.

I asked him if he was sure, and that he wouldn't offend me if he gave me areas of improvement or topics to continue to learn to make myself an even better employee. He said he truly didn't have anything for me to work on, that I was, "Killin' it." This is how every single review discussion went with this boss. He never gave me constructive feedback.

I will give credit where credit is due, though, as he did offer me stretch projects and assignments that I had no prior experience with because he knew I'd figure them out and learn what I needed to learn to make sure they were successful. (These opportunities came from a massive amount of white privilege, for sure.)

I do, however, look back and wish he would have given me some pieces of actionable feedback. I have found that I rarely, if ever, got additional feedback when doing a great job. And in my professional career, I observed that to be true among other women. But men do get actionable feedback. Men not only tend to get the compensation they advocate for earlier in their careers and throughout, but they also tend to get more feedback that is helpful and actionable, which then allows them to work their way up in an organization easier.

Feedback is tough. It's crucial, but tough. And the person giving it really should be equipped to do so, and the person receiving it should be properly prepared to do so based on their preferences in how they process information.

Feedback—in its best form in the business world—is a conversation between two people who have a vested interest in the relationship, whether that is a manager or colleague with the person. Both sides need to understand that feedback is going to be given and heard. Both sides need to prepare. And both sides need to care.

But in order for most people to both give and receive feedback, a layer of trust has to be in place first. Feedback given without trust is just words that bounce off of people and land in the ether.

Don't forget, though, that respect is also needed, and so is psychological safety.

With trust, respect, and psychological safety, feedback can be a gift. It can be the lightbulb that allows different dots to connect for you. It can be a common understanding of where you both are. It can be a stop on the road to a long and healthy relationship that isn't based on yeses and enablement but true understanding and betterment.

Feedback, done wrong, though, can be downright horrible. And feedback given by managers who don't know their employees, don't have trust in their employees, or don't listen to their employees is a different kind of wrong. It's what makes most people go into a flight or fight mentality when they hear the word.

In fact, I'd venture a guess that most people would tell you that the term *feedback* makes them cringe and feel some kind of way that isn't good. Feedback is based on communication, and to be honest, most humans suck at real communication. Most humans don't actively listen. They simply listen to find a gap in order to add their two cents. Feedback is a conversation; it requires two active listeners who care about one another for it to be a successful conversation.

Sometimes *feedback* is used as another word for complaint.

Sometimes *feedback* is used as another word for grievance.

Sometimes *feedback* is used as another word for racism, sexism, misogyny, or any other type of hatred toward someone for something they can't help like their skin color, ethnicity, gender, sexual orientation, etc. But to be very clear here, none of those are the proper, correct, or even okay use of the word *feedback*. Feedback in its true form is none of those things.

In a lot of organizations, feedback is based on broken performance review systems. Performance reviews themselves are broken because most of the metrics and characteristics that are measured and attained are primarily characteristics that men get applauded for and others get denounced for. In other words, performance is based on what the patriarchy has told us is important.

Take aggression for instance.

Aggression, to me, is the readiness to confront. Confrontation. Executives who are men do this all the time, to each other and to women and nonbinary folx. But when a woman confronts a man, whew, look out! They get labeled as man-eaters, man haters, bitches, witches, etc. Men, on the other hand, are rewarded for aggression. Men are rewarded for competitiveness. They are rewarded for ambition. Women are vilified for both competitiveness and ambition. Not just looked down upon, not graded one level lower—vilified. Ambitious women are called cold. Competitive women are called "too much."

But what do all of these double standards scream to me?

It's giving… insecure-leaders-who-have-no-idea-what-they-are-doing-that-are-completely-intimidated-and-terrified-of-the-people-on-their-teams-and-the-people-they-are-colleagues-with vibes.

I'll also let you in on a little secret that many people don't realize, but once you hear it, it may help with some of this ridiculous feedback you may receive; you don't have to accept feedback. You don't! You are not obligated to.

> Women are vilified for both competitiveness and ambition. Not just looked down upon, not graded one level lower—vilified. Ambitious women are called cold. Competitive women are called "too much."

You do not have to accept the feedback that someone who knows you only for a few hours a week during meetings gives to you. You can hear it, but you do not have to accept it.

What if a manager is giving you feedback about a process, or a piece of technology, and how to do it better? Sure, maybe consider that feedback. But what if you have a manager who you feel does not have your best interests in mind and doesn't check in with you enough to know how your work is actually going? You absolutely do not have to accept feedback from that person. They don't know enough about your work to know if you are doing a great job.

And to be fair, feedback is highly subjective. Many people will tell you that it's objective, but it isn't. The thing about feedback is that we are each taking the definitions of words

> You do not have to accept the feedback that someone who knows you only for a few hours a week during meetings gives to you.

and metrics used to gauge people, and we are each interpreting those differently. And then we are also interpreting our own perspective of another person's work.

I mean, if we can't even as a society say whether a dress from the internet is white or blue, how can we possibly try to be objective about feedback?[21]

And the real problem with feedback? Well, we've already seen this play out: feedback then becomes performance and for many people in URGs, the performance-based feedback becomes the one reason a manager needs to *not* give you the promotion or the raise you deserve.

The same goes for references.

References are just feedback after the fact.

Let's stop asking for references. They input even more bias into an interview process, and let's get real, we do not need more bias as humans. We all already exist with some just by being human. We don't need more; we just don't.

But what if we look at feedback not just at an individual level but also across an organization?

Take employee engagement surveys for instance. They are, in their simplest form, the feedback from

> References are just feedback after the fact.

employees of an organization to its leaders. And the problem with most employee engagement surveys is that they are not nuanced enough to ask the right questions, and very few people actually feel comfortable saying what they really feel about an organization anyway, which is why many of them have to be anonymous to get even an ounce of authenticity out of the majority of employees.

And business leaders, for goodness' sake, please stop giving employee survey after employee survey every quarter, every six

---

[21] https://en.wikipedia.org/wiki/The_dress

months, every year, just to not do a damn thing to change the work environment.

We all know that if you ask someone once for something, and you don't take their input, they are hesitant to tell you again. If you ask someone something three times, and they know you aren't going to do anything (or anything of substance) to make a difference, they are going to stop telling you anything.

If you ask me, employee engagement surveys are on their way out. They just don't deliver value anymore because the social contract between employer and employees has changed, and employees trust employers less and less. Which then leads to less engagement and active disengagement, which adds to turnover, which adds to loss of money, which adds to less profit. Until we can bring back employee/employer trust, surveys are garbage because they are mostly based on what people think they *should* say.

So what should you do instead? Instead of performance reviews and instead of employee engagement surveys?

It's really quite simple. Talk to people. Often.

It's the same thing that anyone will tell a business: Talk to your customers early and often.

Well, business leaders, your employees are also your customers. Talk to them early and often. And about real shit, not just scripted and innocuous questions.

> Stop giving employee survey after employee survey every quarter, every six months, every year, just to not do a damn thing to change the work environment.

This is also why it is so important to properly resource the People team. The more people you have in the organization talking to people more often, the more you actually know what the real pulse of the organization is. Not just a small glimpse from three months ago that probably is nowhere near what employees feel today. And let's be real, the People team is never ever resourced appropriately. (More on this later.)

One thing business leaders often forget, and it bears repeating, is that culture changes all the time. Culture is made up of people, and if the people change, the culture changes.

I've always said that a company's culture shifts every second of every minute of every day because the people and their moods, motivations, and feelings shift every second of every minute of every day.

> Culture is made up of people, and if the people change, the culture changes.

Culture ebbs and flows; sometimes it soars, and sometimes it plummets. And where business leaders get into really hot water is that when it plummets, they wait too long to try to save it. The actions they need to execute to save it are the same that were required all along: listening, acting, and making better decisions for the people in your organization.

Feedback is just conversation. We simply act weird and awkward when it's in a workplace setting.

Why do we do that? Because there is a power dynamic, and we need the money from paychecks to live our lives. But don't forget who remains at the top of that power dynamic and would like to keep you exactly where they want you.

> A company's culture shifts every second of every minute of every day because the people and their moods, motivations, and feelings shift every second of every minute of every day.

The patriarchy.

In the Revolution of Work, let's get real with each other so we can deliver *real* feedback so that people, not just white people and white men, can learn, develop, and get promoted into the roles we know they damn well deserve.

Chapter 11

RETURN-TO-OFFICE
MANDATES ARE ARCHAIC

It seems so asinine to make knowledge workers schlep to an office to sit at a desk. Like we don't have desks at home?

Understandably, there are employees who may not have offices in their homes, may not be able to focus on work in their homes, or may need a physical separation from their work and home lives. But to mandate the return to office instead of offering office space as a flexible working option is really idiotic.

Most offices are not great. Even if they look pretty, have ping pong tables in the game room (been there and it's not that great because nobody ever uses them), and have collaboration spots, no one wants to be told where to work when their work comes from their brain. They want to have the option of choosing where they work and when they work.

That's really living the dream, right? Being able to dictate where and when you work?

It's why a lot of people leave Corporate America to run their own businesses or quit to go travel. It's not always the work itself that people hate; sometimes it's the rigid parameters that are placed around knowledge work when it doesn't need to be that way.

There is no necessity for a return-to-office (RTO) mandate. Sure, there are reasons the patriarchy wants you to return to an office. They own the building, pay a shit-ton in rent, they want to show off their fancy offices to friends, or just that they want to be able to see everyone with their butts in seats every day. ("Hi, I'm the word control. Remember me?")

Even as I write this in mid-2023, there is an article every other day on LinkedIn and across media channels detailing that one CEO or another is pressuring employees to return to office.

So here we are, three-year-post-COVID-pandemic start, and we haven't learned a thing. We continue to have oblivious business leaders requiring workers to commute to offices multiple days a week, and employees reluctantly doing so because of the economic forces bearing down on them to stay put in those roles.

During COVID, people took the time to think about what really mattered to them, what was important to them, and how they wanted to spend the next years of their lives on this earth. You'd think business leaders would have gotten the really large, really glaring, really red hint. But they didn't.

Remote work helped disabled communities push to the highest level of employment in recent history, and it allowed for single parents to find more fulfilling roles that worked with their schedules.

Remote work was also far better for those in URGs because they didn't have to deal with Karen's off-handed comments or Kevin's weird and condescending nicknames.

Working remotely even cut down on commutes which cut down on carbon emissions from gas-powered cars which in turn helped the environment.

And parents and caretakers got to see more of their children and their loved ones during the week, a small silver lining in the ridiculousness of the world around them.

> During COVID, people took the time to think about what really mattered to them, what was important to them, and how they wanted to spend the next years of their lives on this earth.

You'd think that leaders would have been all in for increasing both their pipeline of talent and creating better work environments by keeping remote work in place, even if they had to break rental and lease agreements, because they were listening to their employees as humans and doing what worked best for them. But they didn't.

The movie *Office Space* still holds up today for a reason, and the reason isn't a good one. It's because work still sucks for most

---

people, and the movie showed a small iota of what still holds true today.

The future of work still centered around an office, really, for the majority of that time. But in the Revolution of Work, sorry, we're not sorry, that's not going to fly.

Women are far more likely to want to remain remote in their working environments and not go back into an office setting.[22] One study found that only 3 percent of Black workers wanted to return to full-time on-site roles, while 21 percent of their white peers wanted to.[23]

These statistics show that the working environment in offices really isn't working, no matter how many white men are trying to force us back there. I mean, if you were being dismissed at every turn, would you want to go back? And after the brutal murders of thousands of Black and Brown lives over the last few years, and the continued racism that exists in the country today, you'd think that business leaders would have listened and learned about their team members and wanted to help create better workplaces for them, places that ensured their safety. And, you would have also thought that they would have acted on the glaring need to increase diversity, equity, inclusion, and justice in every part of their organizations and businesses, too.

And then they laid off the teams in charge of DEIJ.

So, in the last five years, we've all learned that we would prefer to work remotely (or at least have the option to do so the majority of the time), that we don't want to be in cubicles with eyes on us all day, and that we should be doing more with DEIJ, not less…

---

[22] https://hbr.org/2022/05/why-many-women-of-color-dont-want-to-return-to-the-office

[23] https://futureforum.com/2021/03/11/dismantling-the-office-moving-from-retrofit-to-redesign/

…But the business leaders aren't getting the memo.

I can tell you one thing that a return-to-office mandate signifies to me: those leaders don't give a damn about what employees actually think or want. Because if they did, they would tear up the leases, and start doing what is best for the people in their organizations. I guess these business leaders lived in ivory towers during COVID and weren't affected by any of the same thoughts as the rest of us.

If they did experience an epiphany of sorts at all during COVID, it's certainly not apparent. They're acting like someone accidentally flipped their corporate switches off on their backs in 2020 and just turned them back on this year—kind of like Buzz Lightyear in *Toy Story 3*.

And here's the thing none of them want you to know: They have no idea what they are doing. Not deep down. There is no playbook for going through a global pandemic and then *making* everyone get *back to work* in offices.

They may tout some ridiculous reasoning, but it's slim at best. If they were paying attention at all during the last three years, they would have seen the data showing that productivity went up, and that people preferred working remotely or in a hybrid setting.

Now, do I think that we all need to be 100 percent remote for the next phase of work? No, there are caveats and things to think about here, but I 100 percent know we shouldn't be *forcing* everyone back to an office for the full spectrum of their work time. That's ludicrous.

And anyone who tries to is, in my book, utterly archaic.

> If companies did experience an epiphany of sorts at all during COVID, it's certainly not apparent.

Reasons that leaders say they are mandating return to office are around collaboration, culture, and "our team seems disengaged." Yes, they are disengaged, but guess what, bringing them into an office isn't going to help that. What *will* help is properly listening to them; having them feel seen, heard, valued, and respected; and then having proper resources and a solid budget dedicated to actually being the "people-first" organization that you keep touting everywhere (a claim that falls completely flat).

Something more drastic is needed in the way we work. This can't be it, y'all.

Like, really? Return-to-office mandates? That's really what we have come to? That's what's going to save engagement? Four shitty-gray color cubicle walls is what it will take? We really can't get any more fucking creative than that? Wow. I fear for the future of our species.

If you are a leader right now who thinks RTO is a good idea, and one that will save anything other than dollars leaving the patriarchy's pocket, you are kidding yourself. Actually, you're just lying because those of us paying attention know that these office spaces are some of the largest line items on your expense sheet and would be a huge boon to your bottom line if they didn't exist. Yet, you still act like layoffs, reduction of benefits, reduction of perks, and an overall reduction of humanity are the ways forward.

> Four shitty-gray color cubicle walls is what it will take? We really can't get any more fucking creative than that?

There needs to be a shake-up, a revolution, a real cracking of the white business tower to the ground...

...And it needs to be led by the employees because if we leave it up to the CEOs, as we've seen, we'll get more of the same.

Innovation doesn't typically come from the CEO. Innovation comes from a person or group of people internally who want to make change. Innovation comes from lack of choice or a need to change. Innovation sometimes comes from desperation. Innovation, honestly, comes from someone pissed off enough or tired enough to find a better way of doing the same shit.

And so does Revolution.

We need a Revolution of Work where employees have options and choices. We need fulfilling jobs that respect employees and managers and leaders who care about them as human beings and who allow them to feel valued and special at the same time.

The Revolution of Work needs just that: a group of people willing to stand up, say "WE WILL NOT TAKE THIS ANYMORE," and then stand firm until change happens.

Gen Z is doing the most with this right now. They are the ones who are not standing for what always has been.

The rest of us need to follow their lead and make a stand.

Over the last three years, I've had thousands of people in the workforce reach out to me to tell me stories about how they have been mistreated, purposefully discriminated against, maliciously maligned, and horribly retaliated against, most of which is supremely illegal.

> Innovation comes from someone pissed off enough or tired enough to find a better way of doing the same shit.

And these people were just doing their jobs, merely existing as people in URGs who were trying to come to work like the white people and just do a great job. Yet they couldn't when work is so vastly fucked up because the leaders of most organizations are incredibly egotistical and think they can't possibly do anything wrong ever. There is a reason that my dear friend, Hebba Youssef, started a newsletter called "I Hate It Here" about workplaces, and people flocked to it. There is a reason most people fucking hate Mondays and have Sunday Scaries. There is a reason people can't wait until the weekends, holidays, and ultimately retirement. It is because work sucks, and the majority of people fucking hate their jobs and their bosses.

Jump on any team meeting at any company, and you'll likely hear venting about a certain group or person in leadership. Leaders need to realize this isn't working, and it is their job to change it.

Gone are the days that Monday through Friday, nine-to-five hours work. Gone are the days when leaders can see workers' disenfranchisement as someone else's job to fix.

It is now where leaders need to step up and make changes, drastic and significant changes, in the workplace.

If your CEO believes they are always right, doesn't ever want to listen to people, and always has the answers, that CEO should step down immediately. And if that CEO is you, how dare you think this way today?! Send your own pink slip to your organization if you want it to survive and go do some inner work. It's definitely needed.

Leaders need to get it together. And fast!

The layoffs of 2021, 2022, and 2023 weren't because of the economy. They were because of poor leadership, inflated executive paychecks, irrationally overconfident revenue predictions, and over-ambition.

True leaders would have realized the economy is cyclical; if they didn't, then they shouldn't have been leaders in the first place.

Leaders are the reason layoffs have happened more so in the last several years. It's not the economy, and blaming the economy is a thinly veiled attempt at making their misled actions seem more reasonable.

I'm so tired of us giving leaders the most benefit of the doubt when they should be given the least. They should have the most experience. They should have the most expertise. Hell, if they don't know how to do these things, then they shouldn't be where they are today! If they don't know these things, they need to go back to school, dive into some books, research the economy, learn more, etc., *not* lay people off because of their own short-comings.

And I've been there. Being an executive is hard, of course, but with an increased level of power and authority also comes an increased level of accountability and responsibility.

We live in a society where *blame* is a cuss word. Leaders rarely take blame anymore. Leaders rarely call themselves out for doing things they shouldn't or leading a company down a path of destruction.

And when we do hear of leaders actually calling themselves out for poor planning and performance, it is almost always followed by an "economic dynamics were out of my hands," or "this is really difficult for me" plus the superficial and performative tears running down their cheeks.

GTFOH. (For those following along and also those that are not, this means Get the Fuck Out of Here.)

Most leaders are making two-to-one-hundred-times what some of their employees make, and they want the employees to feel sorry for them when they have to make a call to end a storm of destruction that they led?

It is your fault, executives! YOU MADE THE MESS!

But you know what?

I've got it.

Here's how we fix this mess: We make everyone spend more money in a shitty economy to come back to the office because the patriarchy still needs to be rich.

(Just kidding. Y'all saw that coming, right?!)

Chapter 12

FLEXIBILITY IS KEY IN THE REVOLUTION

We keep coming back to this thought around work and life. No matter what you call it, there are twenty-four hours in the day, and we tend to spend eight hours of it doing work. Some spend more, some spend less. But most people spend about eight hours.

That means that we have eight hours left to sleep and eight hours left to live.

That seems really depressing.

If you travel or work with people in other countries, you'll hear them say more than once that the US lives to work, while many countries tend to work to live.

Humans aren't meant to really have only eight hours a day for free thought, to explore nature, to be with friends and family, to be by themselves, and to feel, touch, see, and do.

We aren't meant to be in a cubicle, an office, a car, for the majority of our days.

And the actual content of our work is changing. Work itself is being split into segments of skill sets. Roles are becoming more fluid and even convoluted. Marketing is flowing into talent acquisition which flows into HR which flows back to operations, and so on.

We have seen, felt, and heard that siloes in a business never work out for the business or the people in it. But we keep trying to build back the walls that keep the siloes in place, whether we mean to or not.

> We keep trying to build back the walls that keep the siloes in place, whether we mean to or not.

What if we thought about work more like a puzzle, where our departments, our skill sets, and our people can be utilized in different ways and in different areas of the business?

Why then would all of these people *need* to be full-time employees? What would be the benefit of that?

Sure, you could count on them to "report to work" to the same company but can you really? Are full-time employees any more stable than consultants, freelancers, and fractional executives?

And on the flip side, is any company really "stable" to work at? I think we saw that from 2020 to 2023 there was no stable company, what with layoffs happening at both large previously thought to be stable organizations and smaller organizations both in tech and outside of it.

The truth is that job stability was always and will always be an illusion.

We as humans tend to want to have some stability, whether that is in relationships, family, friendships, or work. Most people don't thrive on chaos in all areas of their lives. And we as humans tend to want some sort of routine, again, somewhere in our lives. The way the business world is now after the COVID-19 pandemic is vastly different from what it was before the pandemic. Today, people want more freedom and flex-ibility. They don't *want* to be constrained again because they tasted more freedom in their work, and they liked it. Still, even *more* freedom and more flexibility are needed.

> The truth is that job stability was always and will always be an illusion.

Honestly, people just want to feel in control of their own lives.

One of my favorite movies is *The Holiday*, starring Kate Winslet and Cameron Diaz, from 2006. In that movie, Kate Winslet's character states while out with her neighbor to dinner, "You're supposed to be the leading lady of your own life, for God's sake."

And she's right.

But since we can remember, being in Corporate America has meant that if you work for someone else, you are really only in control of your own life for sixteen hours a day at best. The "work" time has been heavily mandated and micromanaged by business leaders. Hell, most employers think that they "own" their employees' time during work hours. How many of us have heard business leaders say, "I pay them to be here!" And they do to an extent, but they aren't going to be able to do that much longer.

With work moving toward being more skills-based, businesses need to start to dramatically shift how they think about employees. Full-time employees may be the bulk of many businesses, but realistically, should they be?

> Honestly, people just want to feel in control of their own lives.

Here's an example, when you are looking to make a sandwich, do you only use the tomatoes, lettuce, onions, dressing, mayo, etc., on sandwiches alone? Or do you use deli meats, cheese, bread, tomatoes, lettuce, and dressing on a sandwich but also use the lettuce, tomatoes, and dressing on salads, or perhaps in another dish entirely? What about the onions—are they only used raw on a sandwich, or do you also caramelize them to use in a risotto or maybe even a soup?

You can use the ingredients in different ways to make several meals, all satisfying and all satiating your hunger.

Now, let's think about work in those terms.

Every person has a set of skills, ingredients—if you will—in a recipe. By having full-time employees, you are asking each person to use their skill sets for one role in one department, almost solely. And some people may like and prefer that for themselves.

But then there are other people who have skill sets that can be used across departments and across functions and across the business, and those people feel hindered by being pigeonholed into just one department or into just one segment of the company. Better yet, there are people who can work across entire businesses and at the same time.

Working in this way can be broken down into a few different avenues, including consulting, freelancing, advising, and fractional work.

Let me break down the differences for you.

Consultants tend to focus in on a scope of work for a limited time period, typically within one department, and they drive outcomes toward a goal set by the strategy of an executive at the company, not one that they came up with themselves. Consultants tend to be more on the execution side as opposed to the strategy side and are hands-on with the project.

Freelancing tends to focus on a very specified skill set that is typically technical, entertainment, art, or design-focused in nature. Freelancers work on a limited scope of a project for a set period of time, or they work with one or two companies at once over a longer period of time.

Advising tends to focus purely on the strategy side of the equation, though advisers can work across multiple businesses at once. They don't typically work on the execution of any strategy, and they have time limits with a particular organization.

Fractional leaders do both strategy and execution for a particular department or across multiple departments or the company as a whole. They tend to have had many years of executive experience prior to becoming fractional and can lead as fractional executives at multiple companies at one time. Fractional leaders work a fraction of the hours a full-time leader works and at a fraction of the cost or at a savings of cost because the level of experience they bring to an organization can save that organization from costly pitfalls.

Then, we have gigs, which are more tasks that people can perform when and how they want. Gigs tend to be driving for rideshare companies, delivering groceries, and delivering takeout food. Gigs tend to be as much or as little work as you want to do, and don't need to have a set cadence or timeframe.

More and more people are getting into flexible work arrangements because they can control the majority of their own time.

The employee and employer agreement and relationship is shifting. For years and years, companies have deteriorated trust in the employee and employer social contract, and frankly, employees are getting increasingly fed up with it.

As they should.

Employers tend to take advantage of people as long as people let them unless they truly are trying to be a people-first company from the outset.

More than ten years ago, I started my own consulting and fractional business, and I don't think I'll ever go back. I don't think I will ever return to Corporate America to work for another organization. Nearly every other person I know who has gone fractional or started their own business has said the exact same thing: "I'm never going back."

The metaphor I commonly use for describing this phenomenon is trying to stuff a huge duvet cover back into the bag it came in. It just doesn't quite all go back. The same goes for fractional or flexible work (consulting, freelancing, advising, gig-work)—you can't put us back into the bag.

As I've been writing this chapter, I was just talking to a friend this week about this very thing. He and I connected after years (and COVID) of time flying by and not grabbing coffee or taking the time to call each other, and as we were catching up in the first few minutes of the call, he said, "It's 4 p.m. and I'm pouring myself a whiskey. I block most afternoons off. That's just not something you can do with a corporate job."

And he was totally right.

It's like once you step into Corporate America, a sort of delusion starts to happen. You start to act according to an unwritten standard of behavior that has no real root in anything at all, other than perhaps control and limitations.

Real humans want to enjoy their lives, and in this case, my friend being the whiskey and bourbon connoisseur that he is, he can now embrace and enjoy those at a time that he deems reasonable without having to wait until happy hour or the weekend to do so.

In essence, he is making that decision for himself because he works for himself.

People want more of that. People want freedom to decide how they spend their twenty-four hours. People want the flexibility of truly grabbing their own life by the horns. People don't really want to drive and roam aimlessly while someone else tells them what to do. Honestly, ask ten friends if they want to be told what to do and where to do it. My guess is that nine if not all ten would say, "Absolutely not." When it's working for a company, however, we do it, almost without questioning it. Because that is what most generations have been taught as the safe bet and just what people do.

Really, the safe bet is to bet on yourself.

Name one company that someone could work for, outside of themselves, where if you wanted to make an extra $10,000 a month or wanted a $10,000 raise, you would get it. Not many.

As a consultant, freelancer, adviser, fractional executive, or gig worker, if you want to make more money, you go and make more money. The money you make is based on you, your efforts, and your skill sets. It's not based off of the limitations of one company, and it's not capped. Working for other people will almost always cap your earning potential and minimize the hours you actually get to spend on what you want to do.

It's time for businesses to start thinking that these new pieces to the employment puzzle are advantages instead of pretending they don't exist and pray they go away.

Think about this: If you have consultants, fractional executives, part-time employees, full-time employees, and freelancers, how much nimbler and more flexible can your entire organization be?

Instead of hiring too many people and then doing layoffs, having flexible resources allows your company to ebb and flow with itself. You don't have layoffs because you have flexible resources. You can jump on business advantages in the market because it takes you less time to staff up projects or new pivots, and you can find experts in fields that you need them in without taking sixty to 120 days to recruit full-time employees.

Your business can either be an advantage for you when you embrace flexible resources and working arrangements, or you can go the opposite route and be the slowest, least nimble company out there that takes forever to hire one kind of employee.

I'd rather be the business owner who has options and more levers to pull as opposed to the business owner who is boxed into one type of employment with one lever.

Plus, if you are an early-stage business owner, founder, or CEO, or a venture capital or private equity firm that works with a lot of portfolio companies, you should want every single advantage out there for your business(es).

> Your business can be an advantage for you when you embrace flexible resources and working arrangements.

For instance, most young, early-stage start-ups in pre-Series B rounds can't hire chief people officers (CPOs) because they can't afford them. Perhaps they hire a Director of People or a VP of People and give them the title for a role they will grow into, but they can't afford the experienced CPO who's been there and understands the mechanisms to scale correctly. So hiring a Fractional CPO allows the early-stage company to gain the expertise of a CPO who can help them avoid costly pitfalls along the way as well as help them scale both thoughtfully and strategically. It helps that

Fractional CPOs know how to work with Boards of Directors as well, alleviating some of that burden from a CEO's shoulders.

Not to mention that having a People leader earlier in a start-up has proven time and time again that the company and its people fare better and enjoy their work more, leading to less attrition and more revenue.

> I'd rather be the business owner who has options and more levers to pull as opposed to the business owner who is boxed into one type of employment with one lever.

So what do you say, business leaders?

Ready to throw out the business books of the 1980s and actually think differently and strategically about your business?

Hiring flexible resources is a very easy, very smart first step in the Revolution.

Chapter 13

REVOLUTION OF WORK— WHERE DO WE START?

It is here.

The Revolution of Work.

It's been here, bubbling for years. It's been lying hidden in every employee who doesn't feel like they quite fit in the rat race. It's been there for every working mother who constantly feels guilty leaving her kids for work and leaving work for her kids. It's been there for working dads who really want to take their entire parental leave off but also feel like they can't because it's not supported in their organization. It's been there for every member of a URG in how they are treated, spoken to, evaluated, not promoted enough, and not given enough money. It's been there for every member of a URG that doesn't feel safe in a work environment, both physically and mentally.

Revolutions don't start from nothing. Revolutions don't start when everything is good and things are peachy. Revolutions start from being fed up with injustices and mistreatment.

I've said it many times in this book so far, and I'll say it again: Work is broken.

Work needs change. Work *needs* a revolution. And I'm hoping this book and its contents spur you to want to make steps toward its revolution.

There should not be a structure in society that supports one demographic and specifically one subset of a demographic more than others, but in the US, for far too long, the structure of work has been working really well for white men. But the structure of work has lacked for and worked against the rest.

We don't need to work around the sunshine like farmers do if we aren't farmers. We don't have to work in office environments if we are knowledge workers. We don't have to only work weekdays and put every ounce of work into five days a week when we can have the flexibility to work when we need to or want to get the job done. We don't need to focus on bias-laced merit-based cultures because the merit is never adequately seen if you aren't a white man. We don't need to focus on weaknesses when our strengths are our superpowers.

We don't need to conform to a culture when we can enhance it and add our own sparkle, and expect others to add their sparkle, to what is already there.

There is absolutely no reason for us to continue to work with the white patriarchy at the center of work.

The only reason to do so is for white people and specifically white men to keep control. That was the basis of the structure from the start. It's also the reasoning for the conformity. It's the reasoning behind "culture fit."

We don't need to continue fitting today's work into old-school patriarchal so-called professionalism. So let's stop doing it.

And what you are probably thinking is, "Sounds great, Anessa, but how do we do that?"

Well, we start by actively revolutionizing how we work.

The Revolution of Work will take active engagement and uncomfortable yet purposeful conversation and actions. Just like everything else. Take climate change for instance; if we are all passive, not enough will change to make a difference.

Change and this revolution will take more than passive activism.

Passiveness only exists to make the person who is being passive feel better about themselves, but it doesn't actually make any change.

> We don't need to conform to a culture when we can enhance it.

Today's brokenness stems from an imbalance of power, where mostly white people and mostly white men have had the power and wielded it for their own benefit first and foremost with little to no regard for anyone else. And because the money keeps coming, the power keeps adding up for them.

But with a lot of people and a lot of conversation—and a lot of action—that power dynamic can topple.

And it needs to. It has to in order to drive real equity, inclusion, accessibility, and diversity.

> We don't need to continue fitting today's work into old-school patriarchal so-called professionalism. So let's stop doing it.

Think of it this way: If you have a ball rolling down a hill, and you don't stop the ball, or divert it to another course, or kick it away, it will continue to roll down the hill, faster and faster. You have to get in front of the ball to change its course.

The work to create a better world and a better workplace for all humans, and not just white ones or straight ones or able-bodied ones, is not going to happen with passive activism.

Passive activism adds to white supremacy and xenophobia because it doesn't do enough to stop it, or even deter it in any way. To be clear, passive activism is not real allyship. Too many "allies" say they are part of the team but never actively participate or go out of their way to do work for those they are supposedly allies for and with.

Real allyship requires action, and not just one action, but multiple layers of action consistently to help create change so that there can be more safe spaces for those people in URGs. Real allyship requires sacrifice.

For me, the measure of real allyship is whether you will give not only your time and energy but will give part of your own money and income so that those in URGs can have more. For instance, I've walked away from lucrative contracts because the executives weren't willing to actually do the work on DEIJ practices and just wanted to check a box. For centuries, my ancestors and people who have looked like me have consistently been given more money than those who don't look like me. So, I'm good with giving up income to help others. But this is a very small piece of the pie and more needs to be done here.

As I write this, PRIDE month just started, and instead of more "love is love," members of the LGBTQIA+ community ask allies to do more—to put their time, their energy, and themselves on the line so that LGBTQIA+ members can exist as freely as we do.

Is it really such a bad thing to want all humans to experience life as freely as one particular group has done for centuries?

No, it's not. But those who are in the patriarchal power fear change so much that many of them cling to it so hard they'd break their bones in their fingers before letting it go.

Don't be that person. Be the person who drives change for others.

> Real allyship requires sacrifice.

Work is a place where inconsistencies in treatment happen a lot. You've probably witnessed it yourself if you aren't a white man. You probably witness it daily if you are a person in a URG.

If we all move forward to change work, we can do it. And in changing work, we can change a third of our days and half of our waking hours on this planet for the better.

Organizations and business leaders need to allocate real thought and a dedicated budget toward better workplaces for all humans, putting emphasis on the right things, not just the easy things.

One of the added problems is that lots of business leaders focus on control and "maximalist protection," as my husband calls it, where companies are so scared of litigation and legal recourse that they focus too much on compliance and not enough on the people.

That shit doesn't work. Because what always happens is a revolt against the business leader. Fear is never a great motivating factor in the end or along the way because fear causes a fight or flight mentality, leaving employees doing maybe half of what they are capable of doing in more supportive environments. So sure, if you want to go with fear, just know you are paying money for half the output. This really seems like one of the most ill-advised business decisions that any leader can make, and I believe if that's your decision as a business leader, you aren't a good one.

And by the way, all of the "things" that you think mean something in the business world? Yeah, they don't really mean much of anything. What do I mean by that? Well, the Ivy League degrees, the paid certifications, the plaques on the wall—none of those mean a damn thing if the person is a shitty person. In fact, I'd rather work with a bunch of amazingly kind people who never went to college and have zero certifications. And to be fair, the Ivy League degrees are a sort of ick-factor themselves because the slots to even be considered at those universities are supremely limited if you aren't a legacy admission, don't have a wealthy family to pay the ridiculously high costs of admission, or weren't picked to be one of very few scholarship students which then also makes those students feel "othered" and tokenized. They look around the room and see way fewer people who look like them and way more who don't look like them. Even attending college at all requires a certain level of privilege, and if there is no privilege to get you there, then it requires major sacrifice. Paid certifications are the same way—if you have the money and the time to study for those, you have levels of privilege, and not everyone has that.

As we look toward the next five, ten, twenty, fifty years, we are going to have to stop thinking in terms of centering whiteness and what white men set as the structure all those many years ago.

If you think about it, there is a major unwillingness for a lot of companies' leadership teams to actually put effort, time, and resources into diversity, inclusion, accessibility, equity, and justice efforts because the structure is working *for* them, so why would they want to change it? We have to strip that thought away. And we have to take action by ripping away "what we've always done" and make changes for all humans that also makes sense for our businesses' long-term goals.

We start the Revolution by starting to change our minds, to change our actions, to change our conversations, and then we can change the way we work.

Chapter 19

REVOLUTION OF WORK—
LET'S START TO
PERSONALIZE

What if we could scrap everything we know about work and start over from scratch? What would it look like?

These questions are the exact ones I asked myself when I knew I was going to write these last three chapters.

What if we actually throw away the patriarchal *professionalism* and ridiculous societal norms that white men put in place and truly start to look at what can benefit more people in doing work they love in environments where they don't have to code switch and can feel free enough to be themselves?

Let's start with—what is work?

For knowledge-based workers, work is taking what's in our minds and transferring that to our work. We may use expertise from previous experiences, work with data, problem solve, synergize with people, create items that weren't there before, etc., but the basis of knowledge-worker work is that it stems from our brains and gets put into practice in some way.

What do we need for work, actually, in this frame?

We need a balance of enough structure to have boundaries in place so that everything doesn't fall into chaos and enough flexibility so that people don't feel constrained.

So what *does* that look like?

Well, honestly, it will be different for every culture and every person. This then leads me to what we actually need in this Revolution of Work—we need personalization.

We have seen nearly every industry go to product personalization in the last decade, from marketing to healthcare. While some industries have far to go, they are all circling around the idea that humans are unique and complicated, and we need different things to thrive.

We don't all love grilled cheese and tomato soup when it's raining and cold outside. We don't all love coffee. We don't all even love wearing sweatpants. (I love wearing yoga pants.)

So why the fuck do we act like we should all be 100 percent happy with working in the same boring space from nine-to-five Monday through Friday?

You don't often hear about boards of directors asking executives if they are in the office, how they are utilizing their time, who they are meeting with and when, when they eat lunch, when they take a bio break, and when they see their families. So why do executives, managers, and other leaders think that's what they should be doing to people who report to them?

If executives have the freedom to work when they travel, work how they want, and work in the way that best suits them, then why can't every other employee do the same thing at the organization, as long as their work is getting done? (And by work getting done, I don't mean while on vacation either. Don't even get me started about expectations on vacation by some bosses.)

> Why the fuck do we act like we should all be 100 percent happy with working in the same boring space from nine-to-five Monday through Friday?

The Revolution of Work will mean freedom to work, and the freedom will come in every aspect of work that we touch right now, and then some.

But that freedom has to be available for *everyone*, as much as we can make it so.

Freedom of work is tied to Revolution of Work because freedom relinquishes the control of few and gives that control to many.

And we need to shift because the younger generation and generations to follow are just not going to stand for all of the same crap that our generation (millennial, remember?) and those before us have. By 2025, we will likely see a shift in the workforce to be made up by almost one-third of those in Generation Z.

Gen Z spent all of their lives online—and now they are moving back toward in-real-life events and trying to minimize screens. Even some say that we may see a shift off of social media by Gen Z and more toward flip phones, sort of like the '90s.

But then will come Generation Alpha. They also have spent their whole lives on screens—from iPads and Netflix shows from when they were very little to Minecraft and Roblox now. When we adults talk about the metaverse, they've been playing in it.

> Freedom relinquishes the control of few and gives that control to many.

Generation Z and Generation Alpha will continue the work that millennials started. They believe in helping the world. They believe in climate change and trying to get everyone to do what we can to shift the human footprint on the globe. They are against bullying because they've had to experience far more bullying from all aspects of life than their millennial, Gen X, and baby boomer counterparts for the most part. And they've had to live life's most pivotal moments while in a pandemic—like growing up, going to school, prom, graduation, etc.

And for Gen Z, they've had to enter the workforce in an economy that wasn't great—something we millennials know a thing or two about because we also entered the workforce in a recession. And I think those similar experiences will bond the millennial and Gen Z generations more than those before us.

Millennials are also not trying to push the next generation down like we so vehemently were. We are trying to help pull up the next generation, not say that "kids today are so entitled" like we were told.

And both millennials and Gen Z want to give back; they want to help the world be a better place. And both generations want to continually learn and branch out to work more on the passions of our lives, not just the work of our lives.

It's funny—we've worked with many start-up leaders who act like their company's mission is world changing when it's not. What if the work of Gen Z's and Gen Alpha's lives is focused on helping to solve world hunger, or finding homes for the unhoused, or trying to clean up the oceans? Organizations working on those missions are world changing. So if your company's mission is not, Gen Z will definitely call you out for that shit as utter and blatant blasphemy. Sorry, they're not sorry. Nor should they be.

And most Generation Alpha members will know more vocabulary words earlier in life than any other generation before them, and they are way more into being unique than fitting in. Their imaginations and innovative minds haven't been squashed and pummeled like those of generations before them. It's going to be amazing to see what they can accomplish.

But here's one thing that won't happen—they won't stand for doing work the same.

Instead of fighting the change in work because "it has worked" for so long—which, like, really? —let's instead look to how we can embrace it and dive into it.

Most of the time, the companies that are at the forefront of these things tend to be better companies earlier on and throughout their existence than companies that wait and lag behind. Have you ever heard of a company doing great that really just waited to see what everyone else was doing, and then jumped on the bandwagon? No, because the bandwagoners become a joke, and for good reason. You might as well get out ahead of it and just maybe you'll find that your employees are far happier, more satisfied, and stay longer.

So how do we personalize work?

I've got a few ideas of how to personalize work. But these are the things coming out of my brain, and I'm sure I'm missing a few items. Consider all of the suggestions I've made in the chapters before this, including compensation, feedback, professionalism, etc., but also consider the following suggestions of what our work *could* look like in and after this Revolution of Work:

1) Increased social responsibility will be at the forefront of what Gen Z and Gen Alpha look for in jobs.

   Businesses should be readying themselves to make a stand for the causes their employees believe in. If companies really want to make people feel safe in their environments, they will need to create safe spaces for them and not donate to causes and groups that try to do the opposite by stripping away their rights bit by bit. Companies should get used to divulging which groups they donate to because employees want to know who their leaders are giving their money to. Businesses should also be readying themselves to be held to higher standards of corporate governance and social responsibility.

2) The line between public and private will become blurred.

   Right now, we live in a world where the number of jobs open far outnumber the number of people to fill those jobs, and that delta will only widen over the next few years. With that, businesses are going to need to get really creative, and the talent pipelines will need to be built in partnership with not only competitors but also between public and private sectors.

3) Business leaders will need to get way better at communication.

   a) Over-communication is going to be key, especially as businesses continue to be more and more remote and move away from office spaces, and especially as people gain more flexibility in the timing and cadence of their work. Gone are the days where mystery can live behind closed doors when it comes to company financials, company plans, and how things are going along the way.

b) Businesses will also need to rethink how they communicate their company's core values because most core values today are seen as top-down and thoughts from the ivory tower, not something that each and every employee or many employees actually live and breathe. Core values should be driven from the bottom up, and business leaders should listen to their employees annually since the culture will shift and change in that time.

4) Flexibility and freedom are what people are striving for.

People want to be able to do work on their own schedules and in their own time—as long as they are accomplishing what they need to accomplish from a results-and-outcome focus. People also want to be able to work from anywhere, in any time zone. And people are going to want fewer and fewer meetings. People want to show up as they are and as they want to—sweatpants, messy hair buns, ball caps, tattoos showing, green hair, glasses, and all. Businesses are going to need to embrace drastically different schedules for employees and then make sure to build out the teams to support that. Businesses are also going to have to cut way down on meetings by creating better organizational and asynchronous systems because they just take up way too much of everyone's time right now. People want to be able to work from where and what time works best for them, off camera, when needed, without stipulation. We act as if we walk through office doors, and another world exists because it seems that way and feels that way. Businesses need to create more personalized approaches to what works for their employees' lives as opposed to trying to fit everyone into the same time and space boxes.

5) People need time to recharge and reset their minds, often. We must start implementing more sabbaticals and time away every year, not just every five or ten years once someone has been working for an organization for that amount of time.

I've had the extreme privilege to be able to consistently take November through January, and even just December through January, off for several years now. As a business owner, I've made that a priority, which means that my holidays are joyful. They aren't stressful, and more than most, I get to stop and be present in the moment for life's precious times with family and friends without feeling like I need to rush around. We need more of this. We need more companies to understand what people are going through and to give them time that is not connected to technology every year. Because guess what? When people have time to recharge and reset, they are more productive and able to be more thoughtful in their work the rest of the year. And by giving employees the ability to do this year after year, you are allowing them to stop when their batteries are at 50 percent, not at 10 percent, which stops burnout from happening across organizations. When burnout happens, so does attrition. By allowing employees more time off annually to recharge and reset, loyalty actually increases while attrition decreases which ultimately means more money earned as a business leader.

6) People want to create lives that *work* with their bodies and not *against* their bodies, and they want work to have a human experience and not just an employee experience.

    a) People want to be able to get the sleep they deserve that matches up with their circadian rhythms. They want to be able to either rise early and get moving or sleep in and have a slow morning. They want to be able to enjoy breakfast with their kids before school or take their dogs for a hike. They want to be able to dive into deep work between midnight and 2 a.m. They want to be able to take an afternoon off during the week to read a few chapters of a book. They want to be able to have the time to go to the grocery store to buy fresh groceries for a brand-new recipe that they are cooking that night. They want to be able to sunbathe nude on their back deck in the middle of the day. They want to be able to pour a glass of whiskey at 2:30 p.m. and be done for the day. They want to be able to align their work with the movement of their lives, not the other way around.

b) People want mental health support and maintenance. It's no longer okay for business leaders to be able to say that they don't support mental health for their employees. If you are able to diminish mental health by having a bad manager, then you damn sure better be ready to do the opposite by getting rid of that horrible manager and helping the person who had to deal with their ridiculous-ness after the fact. You cannot have your cake and eat it, too. Businesses need to put real thought and money in place to support their employees' mental health because we as humans do spend a lot of our lives at work. Business leaders need to realize that they can't keep ignoring this fact.

7) Women want period, perimenopause, and menopause support because the bodily impacts of these are vast and supremely fit in the not-fun category.

a) Instead of having to hide it or work around painful symptoms, businesses can really be body-friendly and help support time away for these pieces. Some companies I know are even giving women paid days off for their menstrual cycles now, but most businesses are behind. And if you think about it—should they be? I mean women have been having these cycles for as long as we've been in existence. Surely businesses can finally catch up. Homo sapiens have been around for a few hundred thousand years. You'd think we'd have it more figured out by now!

b) Businesses need to start supporting employees during the longevity of their lives that they are there, not just during child-bearing years with paid parental leave. If an employee works for a business through those years and then into perimenopause and then menopause, there needs to be the same thought and care placed upon taking care of the employee in those times that there is for the employee during the previous years.

8) People don't want to keep doing repetitive tasks, and technology is taking those roles over anyway, so we need to repurpose the way we think about the content of some work.

Work no longer needs to focus on just one role in one department. We need to focus on skills and how they are transferable across departments and across the company. We need to work within smaller project groups instead of department siloes. And business leaders need to understand their employees as people enough to be able to properly put them where they can thrive and where it works for the business. Will it be hard? Yes. Will it require constant attention? Yes. But that's even more reason to properly resource your People teams.

9) Stop reducing the budgets of People, Talent, Culture, and DEIJ/IDEA teams and wondering why your business is failing.

People are the number one cost for most businesses. Stop acting like your People leader doesn't directly affect the bulk of your business spending and that they can't directly affect the bulk of your revenue. Business leaders who do not get that your People leaders have the single most important jobs at your organizations are either delusional, highly suspect, or worse, outright idiotic.

10) Stop centering work around able-bodied individuals.

a) There are currently fifty-four million people in the US with disabilities, and some of those are invisible disabilities.[24] Businesses need to work with these people so that they don't feel like they need to hide their disabilities to get and keep a job. Again, personalization is needed for what each person may need that matches with their work—not with the fake walls we put up around what we think work should be, but what actually works and needs to get done.

b) Transportation to and from work can be a several-hour journey and requires time and logistics to set up for those with and without disabilities as well. Requiring people to be in an office when their work does not actually necessitate a singular location to complete it also centers those people who have the easiest ability to get to and from that office. While commuting for able-bodied people allows some to listen to music, chat with friends and family, or catch up on work, the same ease may not come to those with disabilities during the same commute. There is an entire workforce that doesn't always get the same opportunities to be as productive as able-bodied folks.

11) People are not all the same. We are complicated and unique and need different things. Stop creating blanket policies, expectations, and singular ways of working.

a) It is estimated that 15 to 20 percent of the population is neurodivergent, but meetings and current work schedules don't really consider those people. We need to work with people to create schedules and working environments that work for them.

b) If we wouldn't even all order the same sandwich at lunch, or even choose to have a sandwich at all for lunch, why do we think that we should be choosing the way everyone

---

[24] https://adata.org/faq/how-many-people-united-states-have-disability

should want and have to work? If you think about it, we give more credence to people's dietary preferences than we do to the ways they work. When you juxtapose those two together, the idea of only one way to work for all really seems silly.

12) People don't want to do a ton of work around their weaknesses, but they love to showcase their strengths. Stop making people double down on what they aren't good at.

For years and years, we've been told to work on our weaknesses—and we absolutely should be on the EQ (emotional intelligence) side and being accepting of other people and respectful of their uniqueness and cultures—but we shouldn't be having employees focusing on their skill weaknesses. Instead, we should be focusing on what their strengths are. By focusing on strengths, you have more productive and happier employees who are proud of their work, instead of focusing on weaknesses that continue to make employees feel inadequate and continue to lose businesses money. Why would we pay someone for six hours of work on a weakness skill that they don't even like to do when we can pay someone for one hour of work for the same skill that is their strength and that they love?

13) People don't want to feel stuck at work. Stop acting like someone's job is the only job they can get and where they will stay for a decade. Work isn't like that anymore.

Career progression should be a team approach, and what I mean by that is that both the company and the employee should approach each employee's career progression as a team effort. Businesses should be working with their employees to expand their careers in a more active way because employees have limited views into what is open and what will open across the company. Businesses should also embrace the ability to have job rotations and explore new skills and roles based on an employee's interests.

14) People and skills need to be seen more as tools used for different projects as opposed to putting one person in one very rigid role.

Very few businesses have enough flexibility in their organizational structure to be agile enough for our current work environment, for when they need to pivot and shift, and for when they need to reverse direction entirely. The new organizational designs will focus on the business's and the employees' abilities to shift and move quickly. These organizational designs will also need to include a variety of employment statuses, like flexible resources, including fractional and part-time employees, consultants, and freelancers.

15) People who are parents and caregivers want more help and support from their employers.

Businesses will need to stop pretending that parents and caregivers don't exist at their organizations and start to embrace and help them. With most families having two parents who work, yet business hours being the same as they always have been, it has created a really hard dynamic for working parents. This dynamic must change. And with more and more traditionalists and baby boomers retiring, Generation X and millennials will need to step more and more into caregiving responsibilities. Businesses need to lead the charge on both of these dynamics so that employees don't feel like they have to choose between taking care of loved ones and doing great work. Both are possible.

16) People want to know more about themselves and how to work better with each other.

a) Businesses should encourage a well-rounded view of every person in the organization to promote more EQ and self-awareness. Businesses should also stop shying away from having tough conversations around social impact issues, and instead make sure the business is supporting all humans and meaning it. Don't discriminate against people and call it business. That must end as well.

b) People are wanting to figure out ways of working that works for them and makes them feel empowered and enlivened. Use a person's lived experience and their perspective to your advantage as a business. People who have had traumatic experiences, who are neurodivergent, or who have learned skills later in life all come at problems differently. Yet, they all want to feel like superheroes and learn their own life hacks to ensure more efficient and higher quality work. Organizations need to lean into this and allow people to explore different ways of working and thinking with each other.

17) People have many passions, and they don't want to just spend their time focusing all of their waking hours on work. Embrace their passions and intertwine those into their jobs or allow them to have outside influences as the mainstream and not as a secret side hustle.

Businesses to this day have moonlighting policies (where employees can't work for other organizations while employed with them), whether they are understood or written. Why? They're afraid that their employees will find passions outside of work that they like better than work. Well, duh! But isn't that on the business to be better at creating a culture and role/skill that people actually enjoy working in and doing? The answer is a resounding yes. Businesses need to embrace people having multiple passions—and those passions not being all about work is totally okay.

18) People want to work for and with people who are authentic, vulnerable, and kind. Stop putting employees in unsafe

situations. And stop allowing assholes to work in your organization for far too long!

a) More business leaders need to show people who they are in their organization. People don't like working for figureheads. They like working with real people.

b) Leaders need to start creating spaces that are psychologically and physically safe. If the space is not safe enough, the business needs to be working on that constantly.

c) Leaders tend to allow toxic employees who are assholes to others (racist, xenophobic, etc.) to stay too long in their organizations, and some of them excuse and overlook this behavior because these employees make the business money. It almost always creates a toxic work environment for way more people than leaders realize, and it should be taken care of quickly.

19) People don't want you to dictate who they can mourn. Stop putting overly strict parameters around bereavement leave.

a) Throw out your current bereavement policy. How dare businesses dictate which relationships warrant time off for someone to mourn? Just give people what they need. If someone's close friend or immediate family member passes away, they may need a month or two, or time here and there. Let them take it—100 percent paid. Stop dictating who and how one human mourns another. That's super barbaric and archaic, just stop it.

b) The same goes for any loss, including miscarriage or losing a furry friend. Again, stop dictating what people should place their love into.

20) Stop doing unpaid internships.

Just stop it. Pay for your labor. I am not a fan of asking for free work, as noted in the chapter on compensation. If you don't pay the younger generation, you are only adding to the disadvantage they have growing up. Come on, y'all—if you are grown up enough to have a business, be grown up enough to pay for your interns. Pay for your labor. Period.

21) Start considering onboarding as the start of an amazing new human-to-human relationship instead of a cold-business operation.

When people are starting new at an organization, instead of most organizations giving them a figurative hug, they tend to give them a really cold and clammy handshake. Is this really the start of a beautiful relationship? Think about this. If you started any other human relationship, one that you really wanted to last and be productive, would you act this way? Yet we continue to do this with onboarding. Most of the time, onboarding is an afterthought when it should be something that represents one of the very first experiences (outside of the candidate experience) in an organization. We should be focusing on giving new hires maps of the area where they may be working so that they can get to know their surroundings. We should be asking them how they prefer to work, what pet peeves they have, and how they prefer to communicate instead of what T-shirt size they are. We should be considering what wellness initiatives are important to them so we can help them put healthy boundaries in place, so they don't burn out from the start.

22) Start embracing the whole human. No really, the *whole* human, not just a piece of one.

This one encompasses a myriad of items, but one situation that I've seen consistently is when people want to get their hair cut during the workweek because most hairstylists do not work at night or on weekends. So when are hair appointments typically booked? Monday through Friday from 9 a.m. to 5 p.m. Maybe a Saturday if there is an appointment available, *maybe*. And how do most people act when they have a hair appointment? They put up an away message on Slack or email, sneak off to the salon, and return to their work, ready to work an additional two or three hours that day because they went to the salon and feel guilty about it. But why? We are literally taking care of our human bodies. Do we as people really want others to feel guilty about taking care of our human bodies? The same situation can be extended to tending to our nails with manicures and pedicures. Instead of making people feel like they need to hide these things, why are we not embracing them because the humans at these appointments are taking care of their bodies?

If you're a business leader, or an employee looking toward the next five to ten years, these are items to really dive into and consider as we step into the new years of work because the Revolution is here.

Which side of it do you want to be on?

Chapter 15

REVOLUTION OF WORK—
HOW DO WE GET THERE
FROM HERE?

The Revolution of Work has started, and businesses' fates will be determined in the next few years and then consistently after that by how they treat their employees.

But what do we need to see from companies to actually make this shift happen? Because we all know employees are on board. The walk-offs, the mass resignations during the pandemic, the myriad of people leaving Corporate America altogether to start their own businesses—all of that shows that employees have had enough and are fed up.

We've also seen unionization efforts go through the roof. This is consistent with disengagement scores and why we need a Revolution of Work to begin with. It all stems from the fact that the patriarchy still pulls *all* the strings.

Not to mention the millions of people who aren't white who have had centuries of harm and oppression that they have had to battle in the workplace and every other area of life. It has created trauma living in human bodies, and why the hell aren't we doing anything about it?

Well, in the Revolution, we will.

We know the *what* and the *so what*. Now we need the *how*. And I need you to fully understand what this movement will take, and if it's right for you.

Before we get into what it means to be in the movement, we also need businesses and organizational leaders to get on board with the following:

1) We need businesses to realize there is a problem with work. We need them to understand they are accessories to the problem; many are the sole core of the problem themselves, but they lack the ability to see this (this happens more than people know).

   There isn't an organization out there that doesn't have some parts of the same Monday to Friday and nine-to-five structure for knowledge workers. Again, why? Why are we using the same rules that we used when women wore full faces of makeup and aprons and served their husbands drinks when they came home from work? And I mean, if you still do that, cool, that's your vibe and your choice, but businesses shouldn't make us have to do things that have been archaic for decades.

Business leaders have way more influence than they let on. A lot of them throw up their hands and say, "Well, that's just the way it is."

It's not.

And it doesn't have to be.

That's an illusion.

They keep doing it this way because it has shown to be highly effective for the wealth in their pockets and the power they want to continue to wield in society.

They will not be so keen on willingly giving up this power and their wealth, but to change the world, we need to pull it from their hands.

If they don't already understand that the world is getting more and more mixed in terms of backgrounds, ethnicities, race, lived experiences, etc., they will be smacked in the face within a few years. I'm talking about the business owners and leaders. Because when their children and their children's children are the minority in our country, won't they feel some kind of way about that?

There are still way too many white business owners and leaders who only look out for themselves, their families, and people who look like them.

2) Business leaders need to release their thoughts of being dictators who *own* their employees.

The power dynamic is way off right now between businesses and employees—and it shouldn't be that way. It should be a fifty-fifty contract, like any other adult relationship aims to be. Businesses still think that they *own* their employees' time. Are we really talking about "owning" anything about a person? Really? Because that worked out so well in the past? Give me a fucking break.

Give it up, businesses. You only pay knowledge workers for their expertise or skill sets. You do not under any circumstances *own* their time.

And you sure as hell don't own their passions, their life's purpose outside of work, who they should bereave, and what their hobbies are. You are not their parents, their partners, their mothers or fathers, their landlords, or their deity. You are exchanging money for a skill—that's it.

Let employees live their lives. And guess what? If you let them live theirs more fully, you as a business leader can also live yours more fully. It's a win-win situation.

3) Chief people officers need to be the leaders of this change and the activists within their organizations. If you don't have a chief people officer, a vice president of People, or a head of People, and you have more than fifty people, get one. Until then, this falls to the CEO or COO—and again, please get a fractional CPO because People are not your expertise, no matter how hard you try. You may think you are doing a good job at leading People, but really you are just playing house with it. Unless of course the CEO or COO was a CPO previously.

> Let employees live their lives.

Chief people officers should always be challenging the status quo in an organization. I'm going to say it again. Chief people officers should always—read: every day—be challenging the status quo in the organization. It is their job. They are there for the people. If they aren't there for the people and they aren't challenging the status quo, then they shouldn't be chief people officers. CPOs should constantly be pushing for a better tomorrow for each and every employee in that organization. CPOs that are yes-men, yes-women, and yes-nonbinary-folx should not be CPOs; that's detrimental to everyone. If you are currently a CPO, and you haven't disagreed or pushed back on your CEO this week yet, or even this month, or heck, this year—you really need to take a long hard look at yourself and ask if your organization is absolutely 100 percent perfection and every employee is 100 percent happy. If the answer isn't a "fuck yeah they are!" then you need to do far more work to move that forward.

And by the way, I'm going to say it again for those in the back…

…If you're in HR, People, Talent, Culture or you manage people in any way, you absolutely need to stop holding up the status quo, and in order to do that, you absolutely must fucking push back. And you must do it often. Stand up and create change in your organization.

The time for excuses is gone. Excuses make things easy, but they don't make it right. Excuses are what hold us back from doing great things that help people. Excuses are when our own trepidations hold us back from doing what is right. Stop the excuses. Excuses harm people because they don't allow you to do the things you need to do to make change happen. Excuses add to keeping the patriarchy in place.

HR, People, and Talent leaders have a responsibility to the people in their organizations. They are the eyes and ears of the lifeblood of the organization. I liken it to heart surgeons—without them, you wouldn't know what is wrong with something so imperative to your body working efficiently and have the ability to fix it. It's the same for people leaders; you are the heart surgeons in your organizations. You must find the delicate balance between being strategic enough to help the business grow and considering the thoughts, feelings, and well-being of all of the people inside the organization. This role is not something to take lightly, and if you got into HR to be a paper pusher or to tell people no, then I'm sorry, but you are in the wrong job. Sure, there are laws and regulations around what companies can do, but it's the People leaders who guide the other leaders of the org through those—and keep the actual employee experience in their minds when they do their work. The laws and regulations are the baseline, not the ceiling. You must stick up for yourself and your team and the people in your organization, all day, every day. I've heard so many People leaders say they have to "look the other way" or "stick their heads in the sand" just to get through their workday. Who is that helping? It damn sure isn't helping you *or* the people in your organization. It's likely only helping the people at the top, which, for most organizations, is pretty lily white if we're really honest with ourselves or paying attention.

What if all of us in People, HR, and Talent said, "No more!"

What if we said, "We are done with this bullshit that each and every one of us has to deal with on a day-to-day basis, trying to push up the hill the boulder of executives actually living their buzzwords and doing the right thing"?

A very amazing woman recently told me that her perception of what I'm all about are these two things: "Cut the bullshit. And do the right thing for your people."

I hadn't thought about my approach that way, but she was absolutely right. (Thank you! You know who you are!)

But it's true! It's not actually difficult to do these things in organizations if leaders would cut the bullshit, get past their own shit, and just do what is right for their people, which by the way also means it is going to be better for their bottom line.

We hear so many business leaders saying they want to be people-first organizations, but their actions are everything that goes against that. And then they wonder why their runway is so short, their people are flooding out of the organization, and no one trusts them?! Huh! It's because they spew bullshit at the wall and hope some of it sticks and turns into money. (Again, it is this way because it serves them to be this way.)

> "Cut the bullshit. And do the right thing for your people."

But People leaders can help this! If we all—I mean *all*—stand up and say we aren't doing this stupid thing because it makes no sense for our people and doesn't in any way make us *people-first* as you all like to say, we can make real change that sticks. But we have to have gumption. We can't be afraid to be laughed at, cussed at, thrown out of rooms, and thrown out of companies.

Because at the end of the day—do you sleep better knowing you did what a white man told you to do, or do you sleep better knowing you did what was right for the people in your organization?

And trust me—I get it—some of you need a job. Cool. Keep on keeping on until you find your next spot, but don't wave the white flag without even trying. It gives us all a bad name in HR (one we are working our way out of!), and it undermines all of our credibility when we are trying to do good work.

If we as a whole each take ten steps forward for the people in our organizations, then we will have helped millions of people.

Surely that's worth a tough moment in an executive meeting or two.

There is a reason that office buildings in cities are being converted en masse to apartments, condos, and coworking spaces. It's not because people standing up against their employers to return to the office isn't working—that shift in the real estate market is happening BECAUSE people stood up and said, "No more." We need more of that. There has never been an easier time to get a message out quickly to people all across the country and all around the world through social media. And I won't say that there has never been more wrong with work because that's not the case, but we truly are not even half as far as we should be with regards to work working for everyone as we are in 2024.

And if we don't stand up, speak out, and do something now to change how we work, we may lose this brief moment in history that is about to develop. But it will take nearly all of us to do this. And we can't do it alone.

4) We need business leaders to wake up and help out, even if it means they lose power. And in order to do this, businesses should double, if not triple, People and Talent team budgets.

For too long, business leaders have thought of People and Talent teams as support functions and given them the budget as such. That's not the case and hasn't been for more than a decade. People and Talent teams lead with the leanest part of the organization in most businesses, and as we move to the next five to ten years, more and more will be asked of the function and industry, and more will need to get done. And CEOs and COOs don't have the skill set needed to perform the tasks that will become absolutely necessary. So, give your People and Talent teams the resources that they need to do a great job and take care of your people. To date, I have never met one CPO or People leader who has felt like they have enough budget and resources to adequately do their jobs—not one!!! That's telling because I know thousands and thousands of them. Give them the resources. Give them the budgets.

And need I remind you how many of you all freaked out when COVID started? Or how many freak out when the market drives a talent war? Then who do you come to? Oh, that's right, you come to the People and Talent teams. Remember that.

Oh, and one small thing here for leaders—centers of excellence (COE) will not work for People or Talent teams moving forward. (A center of excellence model is where an organization has one center that incorporates HR, finance, and other "support" functions—notice how I put them in quotes because those functions aren't support functions if done right—into a group with sort of a dialing in mechanism like a customer service team with a credit card company. In a center of excellence, most employees do not know who they are getting in that COE, and the employees in the COE don't typically know the people or the team the person is speaking about.) A lot of companies try to center this control and mechanism within the organization, but with more personalization and customization being required in the next ten years of business, and with more requirements to be dialed into each and every human's experience, a COE just doesn't get to the heart of the issue or the problem because those in the COE can't possibly know all of the context and the people involved to make the right call. It's the reason most of them have to call in HRBPs (human resources business partners) and geographical or department help anyway when issues arise. So if they already have to pull in double the people to do the work and are duplicating efforts, *and* the COE doesn't have the full picture ever, tell me how these COEs are more efficient and better for the business? I'm pretty sure no employee who has had a COE for their HR team has ever felt taken care of. In fact, the opposite is mostly true. Most employees who experience HR through a COE find it cold and find the people out of touch.

5) And once People and Talent budgets are doubled, we then need real executive partners.

Executives and business leaders, please stop putting down the People and Talent teams. We need real partnerships to be happening. Because let's get really real for a second—who do you call when shit hits the fan, and you have an issue with an employee? Do you clean it up yourself? Hell no! You call HR. Hmm, so if we are the ones you call in a crisis, shouldn't we have your partnership when we *aren't* in a crisis? That's what I thought. Businesses who partner with and elevate People and Talent policies experience less turnover, higher employee engagement, and increased company loyalty. So tell me why you don't want to partner again? If you are a good business leader, it just makes good business sense. But please don't ever forget that *we* are the experts in People and Talent, not the CEO, not the COO, not you—it's us. We know how to do these things. Act accordingly and stop trying to squash our industry as a nice-to-have in the business when frankly it is the *only* thing stopping most of you from getting sued more often. Watch what happens when you truly partner with People and Talent. Magic can happen.

The time to stand up and say that work needs to change is right now. We are at a point in time where our country has seen pendulums swing back and forth from hiring frenzies to layoffs and back to hiring frenzies, but the work world will settle out.

But here's the thing—it won't and can't be the same work that we had pre-COVID. It shouldn't and it can't for economic, societal, and individual family reasons.

Now that you know some of the *why* of why work is so messed up, why we need to change it, and how you can change it, it's your turn to do something with that knowledge.

If you're an employee, go forth and continue to demand what works for you to do work your way.

If you're a business leader, it's time you got with the times and stopped living in the '50s.

If you're a CEO of a business, it's time you stepped up to really change the way you and your employees work, or it's time you stepped down.

It's time.

And if you want to be on the right side of the Revolution, there are some things you will need to acknowledge and agree to, and then be prepared to do. We need people in this Revolution who don't want to just tweak what's been in place for so long, because it's too messed up. There's too much destruction. There have been way too many wrongs.

We need people in this Revolution who aren't afraid to completely burn down the way we work today and to reimagine, create, and enliven the way we all can work better in the future, building it from the ground up.

We need people who aren't afraid to do hard things. We need people who are committed, even when it's exhausting (after a recharge of course). And here's the thing: We need white people to step the hell up and say, "I'm sorry that I've helped to add so much destruction to the way this country has worked for far too long," and then change their daily actions to make it better for others.

If you want to be a part of the Revolution of Work, you must:

- Be ready to look at your own biases, your own actions that have caused harm, and your own actions that have held up the patriarchy in our society (if you're a white person).

- Be ready to get vulnerable and real with conversations and with people. We are all learning, but to actually learn requires vulnerability.

- Be ready to look at your day-to-day routines, how you may be adding to the patriarchy with them, and how you can change that for the better.

- Be ready to talk about the inconsistencies with how different demographics are treated.

- Be ready to actively do something. We can't just have bystanders.

- Be ready to say the hard things out loud.

- Be ready to stand up for what is right for humans, not just white humans.

- Be ready to be a true ally to those who don't look like you.

- Be ready to sacrifice to be a true ally.

- Be ready to have hard conversations with coworkers, friends, and family.

- Be ready to question propaganda used by the patriarchy to try to box you in.

- Be ready to get creative.

- Be ready to embrace all of the possibilities of what work *could* look like and have an open mind.

- Be ready to be respectful of lived experiences from a myriad of perspectives.

- Be ready to drop what you know about how the patriarchy views professionalism.

- Be ready to throw traditional HR out the window.

- Be ready to talk about equity compensation, not just equality compensation.

- Be ready to open your mind to continuous learning and feedback loops.

The Revolution of Work is here. It's going to be hard work. It's going to take effort. And it's going to take a lot of us to make this happen. But if we pull it off, it's going to be worth it, for generations and generations to come.

I mean, unless you want your grandchildren, your friends' grandchildren, and your family's grandchildren to experience the same burnout, disengagement, and hatred of work that we all experience today multiplied by ten or one hundred.

No?

Okay then, what are you going to actively go out and do today?

About the Author

Anessa Fike is a former journalist turned People, Talent, and HR Executive who has led more than 120 organizations across the world. She is CEO and Founder of Fike + Co, a boutique consulting firm that specializes in interim or Fractional People, HR, and Talent Executive Leadership with companies that are experiencing growth, scale, transition, or transformation. Anessa has become an industry leader in all things People and Talent, and she isn't afraid to push the envelope when it comes to speaking up and speaking out. Being called a true ally by many, she has also been named to the Most Inclusive HR Influencer list over many years, has been a product advisor for multiple HR Tech companies, has been a keynote and panel speaker at regional and national conferences, has been a guest on many industry podcasts, and is an IDEA Practitioner with NASA. Her mission—and the mission of Fike + Co—is to help companies build or course correct to create workplace cultures that allow ALL humans to thrive.

To Learn More

If you were inspired by this book and want to work with Anessa Fike and her team at Fike + Co to create a better workplace and work environment, please reach out through https://www.fikeandco.com/ or DM her on LinkedIn at:

https://www.linkedin.com/in/anessafike/

If you are inspired to be an active part of The Revolution of Work and want to kept up-to-date on our TRW Think Tank, TRW city events, and other TRW events, please sign up at:

https://revolutionofwork.com/

Acknowledgments

This book was an effort of love, fueled by the rage of how work has sucked for most people in our country, especially those who do not look like me.

To my husband, Tyler, thank you for not only being my better half, my People leadership thought partner, the spreadsheet guru to my "I hate spreadsheets," and my forever supporter, uplifter, and empowerer. I love you. You always push me to be a better version of myself, and you always encourage me to sparkle as brightly as I can.

To my son, I hope that this book and my work spurs a revolution so that when you get into the working world, your experience is far superior to what people endure today. You are the absolute best thing I've ever done in my life. You are magic. I love you so much!

To my best friend, Tiffany, for always understanding where I'm coming from and being my sister in life. We were somehow born from two different wombs but connected as family. I know that you will always tell me the truth in a way that is kind and comforting. My fellow Virgo, you and I can talk without speaking and can almost telepathically know when the other needs support. I love you, and I love that we can support one another with pure celebration and elation as we continue to show this world just what we can do.

To my parents, Randall and Kathleen, you have always told me how proud you were of me, and you always pushed me to be as spectacular as I could be. I had such a wonderful childhood that was based in the magic that you both made possible. You instilled in me ambition, hard work, and the need to help those who aren't as fortunate as me from a very early age. And mom, you showed me what a strong woman looked like (as did Grandma Helen and Grandma Fern). And thank you both for encouraging me to write. It seems to have worked out! You both also showed me the world throughout my childhood, which gave me a perspective of other cultures that intertwined compassion and empathy in my soul. Thank you for everything you both have sacrificed for me and everything you have done for me. I truly appreciate it, and I love you.

To my Aunt Dawn, growing up, I always felt like you understood me, that you listened to me actively, and that you took what I said seriously. You and Uncle Steve gave me an understanding of art, theater, and culture that has helped shape me into the person I am today. You also have the amazing ability to somehow calm my nerves and anxiety just with your presence. I love you.

To Hebba, you are one in a billion, my friend, and the best ever LinkedIn connection that turned into a real-life friendship. You are someone I know I can always keep it real with and will always tell me if I need to think about something in another way. Your support has meant the world to me, and I only hope I've been the same for you. I love you as much as we both love Rebecca Yarros.

To my Witches and Wolves—Jordan, Mae, and Alisha—thank you for supporting me through laughter and tears, through sparkles and sweatpants, and through great times and hard times. And I can't wait to see what we all accomplish together and individually. Our connected friendship is one for a lifetime and beyond. I love you all.

To my Legendary Ladies—Rocki, Tara, and Rachel—our friendship has been brief but brilliant. The universe knew we needed to find each other, and we've been sisters ever since. I am captivated and humbled by your trust, thoughtfulness, support, and love. You are all such beautiful souls that I'm honored to even just know. I love you!

To the amazing beta readers who had hands in helping to make this the absolute best book it could be—Hebba, Nicole C., Nicole H., Rocki, Tara, Rachel, and Casey—and to my amazing book reviewers, thank you all for taking time out of your days to read through this for me and for your thoughtful feedback. I will always cherish your time, and I will never forget your generosity of spirit.

To the colleagues that I consider friends who have reviewed this book, thank you so much. I truly can not thank you enough for using your time on reading the book for me and providing a nudge for others to read it.

To my fellow HR, People, Talent, Culture, DEIJ, and L&D Leaders, there are tens of thousands of you I could include in this book to thank for your constant support and encouragement. You are all amazing, and I hope that we change the world together.

To Alexa Carlin, thank you for inviting me into the Women Empower X world, not only on stage but also with the Imprint. And thank you for believing in this book as an empowerment for women in the future.

To Tascha Yoder at GracePoint Publishing, thank you for listening, hearing me, and being understanding in my vision for this book as well as being willing to take a chance to go against what traditional publishing looks like. I value your kindness and helpfulness in this process.

To everyone else at GracePoint Publishing, including the fabulous editor Laurie Knight, for being kickass supporters of the vision of this book and of The Revolution of Work movement.

For more great books from WEX Press
Visit Books.GracePointPublishing.com

If you enjoyed reading *The Revolution of Work,* and purchased it through an online retailer, please return to the site and write a review to help others find the book.

Printed in Great Britain
by Amazon

46671284R00126